TALKING TO THE DEAD

About the Author

Sarah LeFanu's books include *Despatches from the Frontiers of the Female Mind* (co-editor) (1986), *In the Chinks of the World Machine: Feminism and Science Fiction* (1988), *Rose Macaulay: A Biography* (2003) and its companion volume, *Dreaming of Rose: A Biographer's Journal* (2013 & 2021), *S is for Samora: A Lexical Biography of Samora Machel and the Mozambican Dream* (2012) and *Something of Themselves: Kipling, Kingsley, Conan Doyle and the Anglo-Boer War* (2020), which was shortlisted for the 2021 Elizabeth Longford Prize for Historical Biography.

Throughout the 1980s Sarah was an editor at The Women's Press, and was responsible for their ground-breaking feminist science fiction list. From the 1990s until recently she has been a part-time tutor at the University of Bristol, and she is also an RLF Writing Fellow. From 2004 to 2009 she was Artistic Director of the Bath Literature Festival.

She lives in North Somerset, and regularly chairs events for the Bristol Festival of Ideas, the Bristol Women's Literature Festival and the Wells Literature Festival, of which she is an Associate. She blogs on films at www.filmwatchingwomen.wordpress.com

Praise for *Something of Themselves: Kipling, Kingsley,*
Conan Doyle and the Anglo-Boer War

This biographical study of three writers in South Africa in 1900 is also a history of the first year of the Boer War, and a splendidly well-written page-turner... Sarah LeFanu has already shown her ability to combine scholarship and storytelling... In *Something of Themselves*, she has achieved a classic.
(Jan Montefiore, *Times Literary Supplement*)

Imaginatively conceived, meticulously researched and subtly narrated, *Something of Themselves* is not only a biographical treasure trove but also offers fresh insights into that charged moment when the writing was at last firmly on the wall for old-style British imperialism.
(David Kynaston)

A brilliantly insightful, very moving examination of three writers on the battlefield. LeFanu reveals each of her subjects to be engaged in his or her own private war, at the same time as they participated in the war that came to define the cruelty and confusion of the British Empire.
(Lara Feigel)

This lively and thoroughly researched book gives an effective account of the political and military events of the Boer War, splendidly evoking the geographical and social landscape against which it was fought... Sarah LeFanu brings the story to life...full of interesting extras and witty asides.
(Richard Maidment, *The Kipling Journal*)

In *Something of Themselves*, [LeFanu] places Kipling alongside Arthur Conan Doyle and Mary Kingsley at the center of a fascinating study recounting their experiences in the Boer War, a conflict that all three witnessed at close hand.
(Benjamin Shull, *The Wall Street Journal*)

An ambitious but compelling biographical work... There is as much joy in it for readers as there are lessons for writers...magisterial.
(Uddalak Mukherjee, *The Telegraph of India*)

LeFanu has written a highly original, thought-provoking and insightful study of three great writers at a moment of imperial crisis...a sensitive, multi-layered book.
(Saul David, *The Daily Telegraph*)

Praise for *Dreaming of Rose: A Biographer's Journal*

This is such a wise and charming book, giving us a glimpse over the shoulder of a biographer at work. It captures what it's really like to write a biography, which is nothing like the soothing sensation of reading one...a tribute to biography itself, as a quest, as an art, and as the most generous and selfless of literary genres.
(Sarah Bakewell)

TALKING TO THE DEAD

TRAVELS OF A BIOGRAPHER

Sarah LeFanu

SilverWood

Published in 2023 by SilverWood Books

SilverWood Books Ltd
14 Small Street, Bristol, BS1 1DE, United Kingdom
www.silverwoodbooks.co.uk

A version of the Bloemfontein section of Chapter 1, 'Talking to the Dead', was
published in the RLF online journal *Collected*, February 2016.

Cover photograph of Mary Kingsley by kind permission
of Liverpool School of Tropical Medicine

ISBN 978-1-80042-262-9 (paperback)

British Library Cataloguing in Publication Data
A CIP catalogue record for this book is
available from the British Library

Page design and typesetting by SilverWood Books

For Mon, again, and for my daughters

Contents

Introduction

In May 2015 I travelled to South Africa with a head full of half-formed notions about a book I wanted to write, a book about three British writers at the beginning of the last century and their involvement in the Boer War. I knew who my three biographical subjects would be – Rudyard Kipling, Mary Kingsley and Arthur Conan Doyle – but beyond that I knew very little. This book is a journal of my research for and writing of that story, which was published four and a half years later, by Hurst & Co, as *Something of Themselves: Kipling, Kingsley, Conan Doyle and the Anglo-Boer War.*

When Britain declared war against the Boer Republics of the Transvaal and the Orange Free State in October 1899, the government and press assured the British public that the fighting would be over by Christmas. The Boers, it was pointed out, had no proper army. No one believed that 30,000 farmers – for they were farmers, not soldiers – could stand up for long against what the anti-imperialist Olive Schreiner bitterly called 'the greatest empire upon earth, on which the sun never sets, with its five hundred million subjects'. By Christmas, however, British confidence was badly shaken. A string of unexpected military defeats had resulted in shockingly high casualty rates. Hundreds of British soldiers had been taken prisoner, an unheard-of humiliation. Inside the British territories of Natal and the Cape, the towns of Ladysmith,

Kimberley and Mafeking were under siege by Boer forces. This was the situation that confronted my three subjects when, in early 1900, they disembarked from their steamships in the shadow of Table Mountain.

My fourth subject was the conflict itself. What was it that interested me about this period, this place, this war? I have written about Africa before, in *S is for Samora: A Lexical Biography of Samora Machel and the Mozambican Dream*, but it is only recently that I have come to recognize (or admit to myself) that my interest in African history might be partly related to my own personal or family history. My paternal grandfather – a doctor, who died many years before I was born – went out to West Africa in the early years of the twentieth century, only six or seven years after Mary Kingsley's final West African journey. He spent his working life on the Gold Coast (now Ghana), and returned to England in the 1920s, where he slowly died of the sleeping sickness with which he had been infected. Mary Kingsley was an expert on morbidity and mortality in West Africa, with an unusual (for a European) interest in traditional medicine. In 1908 my grandfather had returned briefly from the Gold Coast to take a diploma in tropical medicine at the Liverpool School of Tropical Medicine, where the Mary Kingsley Medal for research into those diseases – such as malaria, yellow fever and, not least, sleeping sickness – was inaugurated in 1902, and is still awarded today.

My own father worked for the British Council in East Africa in the 1950s and early '60s, and I spent part of my early childhood in Uganda and Kenya, in the years leading up to decolonization and independence.

And South Africa? In my twenties I was involved with a British solidarity group that supported the struggles for independence in African countries that had been Portuguese colonies (or what the Portuguese government liked to call 'overseas provinces'). I spent two years working as a teacher in newly liberated Mozambique; a period of my life that became part of the narrative of *S is for Samora*. The apartheid regime in South Africa was then a powerful enemy. It was implacably opposed to its neighbour's revolutionary aims, and was doing all it could to undermine and destabilize them. Although it has never been officially acknowledged, it is widely accepted, based on both evidence and eyewitness testimony, that South Africa's secret security forces engineered the plane crash in October 1986 that killed Samora Machel along with a number of his ministers and advisers.

Britain's earlier meddling in South African affairs and its aggressive pursuit of an unnecessary war with the Boer Republics at the turn of the twentieth century was something about which I knew very little back then. The subject remains only rarely written about: the war seems to have been swept aside by the torrent of history books, biographies and novels (not to mention films and television series) relating to the two world wars that followed it. Yet the Anglo-Boer War was a turning point, both for South Africa (the war's relation to the rise to power of Afrikaner nationalism and the creation of the apartheid state is still being explored by historians) and for British imperialism. Was it 'a first-class dress-parade' for the Armageddon of the First World War, as is suggested by a British general in one of Kipling's short stories? Or did it foreshadow, rather, the British response to the anti-colonial guerrilla wars of the mid century? I am interested in these big historical questions, but I'm not a historian; I'm a biographer.

How, then, did I choose my three biographical subjects? I have been interested in the life of Mary Kingsley for some time; ever since I discovered that she was a fierce critic of British colonial muddling in West Africa, rather than (as she has sometimes been portrayed) an eccentric Victorian spinster or lady traveller. She writes with a curiously modern-sounding voice: ironic, wry, self-deprecatory. West Africa was the subject of her two big books, and her travels there have been wonderfully written about by Caroline Alexander in an intelligent, empathetic in-the-footsteps account.[1] Kingsley's time in South Africa, where she nursed Boer prisoners of war in a military hospital near Cape Town, was cut short by her death from typhoid, which she had contracted from the men she was nursing. I was curious about what took her to South Africa, and about what she found there.

What were the factors that propelled Rudyard Kipling and Arthur Conan Doyle to this distant war? As with Kingsley, I was interested in what they were sailing away from as well as what they were sailing towards. What roles did they hope to play in South Africa, and how did their experience compare to their preconceptions, to their original hopes and fears? What did it mean to them as writers?

My journal gives an account of what I learned and how I learned it. It is about the biographical process, and it is also about South Africa then and now, about Britain then and now, about imperialism, about travel, and about writing. It gives an account of my search for knowledge and understanding, and my response to what I found.

Place plays an important role in biographical writing. I made two trips to South Africa. The first, in 2015, was to Bloemfontein and very briefly to Cape Town, when I had only the haziest notion of what shape my book might take. The second, in 2018, saw me return to Cape Town. I find, as a biographer, that sometimes my subjects seem most present where they have left little or no trace, in non-urban spaces that have been little touched by the passage of time. I felt the ghostly presence of Kipling and Doyle in the 'enormous pale landscape' (Kipling) outside Bloemfontein, where,

---

1   *One Dry Season: In the Footsteps of Mary Kingsley* by Caroline Alexander, 1989, Bloomsbury.

in March 1900, one of the significant battles was fought between the British and the Boers. Doyle and Kipling witnessed its aftermath. All that marks the site now is a dilapidated war-graves cemetery that is slowly sinking into the grasses of the surrounding veldt. Similarly, as I stood on the steps of the Palace Barracks Hospital in Simon's Town I could almost see Mary Kingsley sitting along from me on the veranda, watching the sun sink into the ocean, clutching a mug of Cape wine in one hand and a cigarette in the other to keep away the mosquitoes. Yet, while important to me, these moments of imaginative empathy or identification didn't find a place in the finished biography.

Nor was there a place in the final text for the archives and libraries – in London, Liverpool, Bristol, Birmingham, Oxford, Sussex and Dublin – where I read letters, looked at newspaper clippings, and discovered the details of my subjects' lives and the events in which they were caught up. Spending time in archives and libraries is part of the biographical work that is invisible outside the footnotes and references of a published book. Those places are way stations along the route of the biographer's journey.

Biographical subjects can be puffed up or deflated, presented in a flattering or an unflattering light, treated deferentially or impertinently, truthfully (the reader is entitled to hope) and/or colourfully. Whatever the current fashion in biographical writing, and whatever the aim of the biographer, the finished biography often creates an impression in the reader of seamless inevitability. The track the biographer has taken in the course of their research and writing may have been (and usually has been) punctuated by surprises, blind alleys, surging waves of creativity, reinterpretations and reconsiderations, and strokes of good or bad fortune. Yet the biographer's twists and turns, their errors committed and their moments of despair, are no more visible to the reader of the finished book than are the false starts, the wrong endings or the mid-work misdirections taken by a novelist, dramatist or poet. Like other writers, biographers sometimes weep, often feel frustrated, and frequently wonder why they ever started on this work in the first place. Some of that appears in the following pages.

My journal entries deconstruct the smooth edifice of the finished biography, and while that biography is informed by my own perspective on my three subjects and on the war in South Africa in which they all played a part (how could it not be?), the journal entries foreground the subjectivity, or partiality, of that perspective. Such a deconstruction of the biographical endeavour necessarily entails the insertion of autobiographical material. All aspects of my life during those four and a half years fed into the book I was writing in one way or another, but some more critically than others.

As you will read, my preoccupation with the work of research and writing ran in parallel with another preoccupation, something that was constantly present and from which I couldn't escape. In the spring of 2016, at the very time when the hazy notions I had about the book I might write were coalescing into a clearer shape and ambition, I developed a chronic and painful autoimmune condition called polymyalgia rheumatica (known as PMR); although the pain is alleviated – patchily – by corticosteroids, the drugs themselves trail problems of their own. Over the next four years, the anxieties I had about my writing and the difficulties I experienced often seemed closely entwined with the anxieties and difficulties caused by the PMR. As with the biography I was researching and beginning to write, I started off without much knowledge of the condition. As the months and then the years passed, what I learned about it was learned not in archives or libraries, but in my body. As the biography was completed and published, the PMR dragged on. I have ended up living with it for a much longer period than I lived with Mary Kingsley, Rudyard Kipling or Arthur Conan Doyle.

As I write now, seven years after the PMR first made its presence felt, it seems to have almost gone. Although its traces, I suspect, are permanently inscribed within me, it now whispers in my body rather than shouts aloud.

Chapter 1

May 2015; South Africa

14 May 2015

University of the Free State (UFS), Bloemfontein, where Melanie Walker runs the Centre for Research in Higher Education and Development. I am here because my old friend and stalwart travel companion (Ireland, Turkey, Mozambique) Monica McLean has come to do a week's work with Melanie. They have worked together on various projects, and co-authored *Professional Education, Capabilities and the Public Good: The Role of Universities in Promoting Human Development*, and Mon suggested I come with her to do some research on my book. My potential or imaginary book, that is, which at present exists only in my head. Two of its subjects, Arthur Conan Doyle and Rudyard Kipling, found themselves here in Bloemfontein during the Boer War. They arrived in March 1900, soon after the town – the capital of the Orange Free State – fell to the British forces when the war between Britain and the Boer Republics was in its sixth month. Kipling was here to co-edit a local paper called *The Friend*, which had been taken over by the British Army, and Doyle was a physician at Langman's Field Hospital. More than a hundred years have passed since then. Will I find any trace of them at all? Mon's offer provides me with an excuse to nose around, to see what I can see, even if I don't yet really know what it is exactly that I am looking for. I always start a biography from a state of unknowing: it is scary, but also liberating.

In return for board and lodging with Mon, Melanie has generously offered me a day of academic writing workshops with her graduate students and those from the history department. They have already filled out the questionnaires I sent them a few weeks ago, and sent me examples of their work.

Mon to Melanie, driving us to the campus on the first morning: 'Sarah thinks the students' academic writing is good.'

Melanie: 'They wouldn't be here if they weren't good.'

Melanie's office manager, Lucretia, could not be more considerate of our well-being. We are settled in the room reserved for visiting fellows – Room 101, no less – in the Benito Khotseng Building.[2] Three desks with padded swivel chairs, desktop computers, the wherewithal to make coffee or tea whenever we want... I can't imagine such a space being made available to visiting academics in a British university, least of all to an unofficial hanger-on like myself.

Undergraduate teaching is in English and in Afrikaans, in separate but parallel courses.[3] The black students (about 80% of the intake) take the English-language route; the white students the Afrikaans one. The two routes are allocated equal funding, and so, with smaller class sizes, the white students end up in a privileged position. I remember that language – the demand of black school students to continue to be taught in English rather than in Afrikaans – was the spark behind the Soweto Uprising in 1976. The vice chancellor, says Melanie, bends over backwards to

---

2   Benito Khotseng was a humanitarian educationist who worked at UFS and at the University of Cape Town, and a visiting professor in the UK and USA. I discovered later that he had died, aged sixty-seven, only four months earlier, in January 2015.

3   This is no longer the case: all teaching is now in English.

'include' the Afrikaner students and to accommodate their every demand. The Afrikaners have become a vocal minority that has positioned itself in the new South Africa as oppressed, beleaguered, sidelined. What they suffered and lost during the Boer War over a hundred years ago remains fresh in their consciousness. In tones of marvellous disdain, Melanie told us of a dinner party she and her husband recently went to at which, when the conversation turned to the Boer War, a fifty-year-old Afrikaner man sitting opposite her started weeping.

Clear blue skies, hot sun, reddish-brown earth, the acacias shedding their dry leaves and papery bark onto the dusty paths that line the streets of Bloemfontein. Wide roads, presumably built originally for farmers' wagons but now busy with trucks and cars, and car dealerships on every street corner. Beggars stand in between the lanes of cars and trucks on the highways near traffic lights and crossroads. One white couple – the woman in a white jumper and dark slacks, her man in a shirt and tie – were also working the stationary lines of vehicles, but they didn't look nearly as poor as the black beggars. I haven't yet seen anyone wind down a window and drop a coin into a beggar's paper cup, as drivers do in Turkey as a matter of course, practical charity being a tenet of Islam.

When Mon and I arrived at the Boa Vida guest house the owner, Olivia, had gone out, and the young woman left in charge expressed surprise that there were two of us. She showed us into a small, dark bedroom which, she informed us in hesitant English, we would be sharing. It was our turn to be surprised.

'Is the room I had last year free?' asked Mon.

Reserved for another guest, the girl told her.

Oh, well. Could we have a sandwich or something?

'No. Kitchen closed.'

Could we get one somewhere nearby?

She drew us a map to the supermarket.

One hour later, tired, dusty and lost, we were hailed by the driver of a car that pulled over. 'This may seem a strange question,' said the woman behind the wheel, 'but is your name Sarah?' It was Olivia, who had heard from her father that he had spotted two dust-covered white women passing his house and then, a while later, the same two women staggering past again, looking even dustier. Olivia had jumped into her car and driven from street to street looking for us; she had even rung Lucretia in a panic, saying that she had lost us.

Returning to the Boa Vida, we were shown to two separate rooms. The room Mon had asked about – a large, airy room with its own kitchen and sitting area – was indeed reserved: for Mon herself.

I was caught up in a similar crossed-wire muddle on campus yesterday morning, when Lucretia kindly took me to meet a woman in the archive centre whom Melanie had thought I might find useful. As we arrived at her open doorway she leapt up from behind her desk, hand outstretched, and said how pleased she was to see us, and that I didn't look at all like my photograph. She had assumed, not unreasonably, that we were the visitors whom she was actually expecting, coincidentally at that very moment. Confusion was worse confounded when the two women she had been expecting turned up simultaneously with a couple of men. It was unclear to me, and I think to her too, whether the two men were in any way related to the women, or whether they were yet further chance visitors. We all stood in a knot outside her door, while she valiantly attempted to introduce us to each other without ever having met any of us before. Lucretia was looking very uncomfortable, but, having been the first to arrive, we were positioned on the further side of the group from our only escape route, and it took a certain amount of manoeuvring to get past the blockage.

When we eventually got out, I said to Lucretia, 'That was quite comic, wasn't it?', and luckily (because I think she gets anxious about things being right and proper), she laughed and agreed. I suspect that on the previous afternoon she had been really quite panicked by the report of our going missing on the streets of Bloemfontein.

I have now emailed a professor of history who specializes in the Anglo-Boer War and whose name I was given by the archives woman just before all her other visitors swooped down on her, but I haven't yet heard back from him. Meanwhile Lucretia called me up a taxi to the Anglo-Boer War Museum, which is a few kilometres out of town. It lies in extensive grounds, and when I arrived I found a bevy of gardeners planting a garden of remembrance around a series of what looked like newly constructed low walls, which had words engraved in Afrikaans on one side and English on the other. These turned out to be excerpts from a speech written by the English anti-war campaigner Emily Hobhouse for the opening ceremony, in 1913, of a monument to the tens of thousands of Boer women and children who endured, and died in, the British concentration camps. Hobhouse fell ill on the journey out to South Africa in 1913 and had to return to England. Her speech was read out by someone else (a man, doubtless), with certain omissions including, I believe, the following, now engraved on one of the walls: 'Does not justice bid us remember today how many thousands of the dark race perished also in Concentration Camps in a quarrel that was not theirs?'

The low walls lead the visitor up to an open space at the foot of the monument. You look up at a larger-than-life pietà: two Boer women and a dead child. Hobhouse had described such a scene, which she had seen with her own eyes at the Springfontein concentration camp, to the monument's sculptor, Anton van Wouw, when she met him in Rome. Despite their size, the figures are dwarfed by an enormously tall obelisk of red stone thrusting into the sky behind them.

Other heroic Boer statuary is on display elsewhere in the museum grounds: a burgher on his pony, Mauser strapped across his back, leans down to his wife and baby for a farewell kiss; an old man and a young boy clutch a railing on the deck of a ship that is taking them to exile in foreign lands; and, positioned on the ridge of land overlooking the museum, a gaunt *bittereinder* (a Boer who refused to surrender, and fought to the 'bitter end') sits on a cadaverous pony.

It was fortunate I was on my own in the museum and not accompanied by Melanie, as I have to admit I was almost crying at some of the exhibits: photos of burned-out farms, massacred livestock, skeletal Boer children dying in the camps. Black men shot as spies – by both sides – in what the British called a 'white man's war' or a 'gentleman's war'. Bullet holes in a baby's bloodstained cotton bonnet. What did I find out? All sorts of things that I hadn't known: that the Boer commandos (as they called their fighting men) conducted what was essentially guerrilla warfare, making sorties from their scattered farms on swift-footed ponies, and taking shots with their long-barrelled Mausers at the lumbering British lines before vanishing in a cloud of brown veldt dust; that the British sent the captured Boers, including men in their sixties and boys as young as ten, to prison camps at the furthest reaches of the empire; that the families of the *bittereinders* were punished in the concentration camps by being given only half of the (exiguous) rations allowed to the families of the *hansoppers* ('hands-uppers', who had surrendered or defected to the British); that many Europeans came to Africa to fight alongside the Boers in an early form of the International Brigades (one of them was thirty-two-year-old Cornelis van Gogh, Vincent's younger brother; he was captured by the British and died in a field hospital in April 1900);

that the funerary ashes of Emily Hobhouse are interred at the foot of the monument in the museum grounds.

The Boers had ponies, Mausers, soft felt hats. The British had blockhouses, barbed wire, concentration camps. I walked around a model of the concentration camp that was set up on the edge of Bloemfontein the year after Doyle and Kipling were there. Cases of guns against the walls: the British Lee–Metford and Lee–Enfield rifles were outgunned by the Boer 7x57mm Mausers – the first modern high-velocity rifle, I learned from the guidebook – but in the end the Boers' type of guerrilla warfare couldn't withstand the scorched earth policy of the two British lords, Roberts and Kitchener.

16 May

I was keen to visit a place called Sanna's Post (or Sannaspos), that Arthur Conan Doyle described in the South Africa section of his memoir *Memories and Adventures*. It is the site of a battle that took place on the last day of March 1900 after a group of Boer commandos successfully ambushed a column of British soldiers. The Boers then seized and destroyed Bloemfontein's water supply. Over the next few weeks more than 2,000 British troops died of typhoid (in his memoir, Doyle gives the much higher figure of 5,000). Doyle, who had come out to South Africa expecting to tend to the heroic battle-wounded, found himself instead trying to deal with death 'in its vilest, filthiest form'. The stink could be discerned six miles away. In one of his poems Rudyard Kipling has his Tommies call the town 'Bloomingtyphoidtein'.

Lucretia recommended I hire a guide to take me to the battleground of Sanna's Post, and suggested an old colleague of hers called Johan, a lecturer in tourism and business studies at the Central University of Technology, Free State (CUT, the technological university in Bloemfontein), and part-time tourist guide. We drove out in Johan's Land Rover, stopping at the site of the concentration camp which is an area of scrubby wasteland behind a chain-linked fence, with a marsh at one end where the women used to do their laundry. In the museum I'd seen photographs of some of the sad processions in which tiny coffins were carried from the camp along the dusty road to the graveyard at the other end of town. We went on through empty countryside. It is so unlike neighbouring Mozambique, where you pass villages dotted alongside the main roads, and always people walking or bicycling from one to another. We saw no one until Johan drew my attention to a fleet of dirty, beaten-up buses rattling towards us. As they passed I caught a glimpse of faces behind the grimy windows: workers, said Johan, being bussed into Bloemfontein from distant townships which are home to the majority of the black population.

Johan drew up on the top of a low incline that looked out over a stretch of flat brown land towards a clump of eucalyptus that, he said, concealed the deserted buildings of the old railway station of Sanna's Post. He pointed out the course of the Koornspruit River below us, marked by a thin greeny-yellow line of willow and sweet thorn, on the dry bed of which the Boer commandos had concealed themselves under cover of darkness. In the morning, as the British gun wagons rolled down to the 'drift' (or ford), the Boers seized their drivers and, disguised in their stolen uniforms, drove the guns up the far bank and away. A fierce battle ensued that left the British with over 500 casualties.

Kipling the journalist missed out on this battle, but Conan Doyle came and scrutinized the battlefield a week or two later. He puzzled over the scattered cartridges of soft-nosed bullets (Boer? British? The use of soft-nosed bullets, or dumdums, had been officially banned), and took note of the vulture-ravaged remains of the 'poor artillery horses'.

'There's something else you might like to see,' said Johan.

We climbed back into the Land Rover, drove over the bridge that now spans the river, and jolted down a dirt track towards the station hidden behind the eucalyptus. Through the rough grass and scrub I caught a glimpse of a low brick wall forming an enclosure of some kind. We stopped in front of a metal gate, hanging half-open, and I saw that inside was a small cemetery. A tarnished plaque let into the wall said that it belonged to the South African War Graves Commission. Inside the gate stood two white marble crosses on stepped plinths, engraved with the details of three British officers who fell in 'the action of Koornspruit' on 31 March 1900. Beyond them stretched two lines of grey basalt headstones that marked the graves of the rank and file. Prairie grass pushed up through the gravel between the headstones. Behind us the eucalyptus rustled in an invisible breeze. In front of us open veldt stretched eastward, unbroken as far as the distant flat-topped kopjes on the horizon.

'Do you often bring people out here?' I asked Johan.

He told me I was the first person this year.

'And last year?' I asked. 'How many?'

'One only,' he replied.

I wondered who that one person was. A distant relation of one of these young British soldiers? Or just someone such as me, interested in the war?

The smallness of the cemetery amidst the vast emptiness of the veldt reminded me of the lonely hillside, some hundreds of miles to the east, where Samora Machel had met his death, and where I'd felt that the ghosts of the dead were within earshot. These bones had lain quietly for more than a hundred years. I could almost see Rudyard Kipling riding his little borrowed pony across the dusty scrub, hoping to witness a skirmish in what was fast becoming a guerrilla war. And I could almost see Arthur Conan Doyle, with notebook and pencil in hand, picking his way between the dead horses and heaps of torn clothing and broken helmets scattered across the deserted battlefield.

Back in Bloemfontein, Johan drove me past the (hideous) red-brick Anglican cathedral where J. R. R. Tolkien was baptised in 1892. I had had no idea that Tolkien had been born in South Africa. By the time war broke out in 1899, his widowed mother had taken him and his brother back to England. Then we drove through some leafy suburbs: grand, gated houses set well back from the road, each one with the same sign fixed to the sturdy metal gate: 'Senforce: Guarding. Armed Reaction. Cleaning', illustrated with a fierce-looking Alsatian dog. The apartheid police used to use Alsatians for law enforcement against the black population – i.e. for chasing, biting, tearing. Except for the white couple who were begging at the traffic lights, Mon and I have seen no white pedestrians since we arrived. All white people (save that couple) drive or are driven; they claim it is the only way to feel safe. The trouble is that if you are the only white people on the streets – as Mon and I often are – you feel you are doing something not normal. And that makes you anxious.

Melanie took Mon and me and two of her Zimbabwean postdocs to lunch at the Oliewenhuis Art Museum, where the sloping lawn is crowded with life-size statues of activists and revolutionaries who over the years have fought for racial equality, social justice and freedom in South Africa. At the head of them, approaching the museum building, is Solomon Plaatje, wheeling the bicycle which he rode around the country in 1913, campaigning against the Natives Land Act which would make the 'Native African,' as he said, 'not actually a slave, but a pariah in the land of his birth'. I had read about Plaatje and seen a photograph of him in the Anglo-Boer War Museum. He worked as an interpreter and liaison between black and white in Mafeking during the siege, and kept a journal (published in the 1960s, I think) that I must try and get hold of. He was a founder member of the South African Native National Congress, later the African National Congress (ANC).

I like the mental powerhouse that is Melanie. She is a pretty woman, slim and smartly dressed; she can be guaranteed to say something rude about almost any academic colleague whose name Mon happens to mention (examples: 'I'd rather die than work with her again'; 'Oh, she's toxic'; 'He only wants to talk about himself'). At first I found her plain-spokenness alarming, but now I'm rather enjoying it. As Mon points out, Melanie provides a refreshing model of a woman academic *not* trying to please other people the whole time, but pursuing what she wants in her own way. More importantly, she is hugely encouraging of her students, and especially empowering of the young women who work with her. Martha Nussbaum informs much of the work she and Mon are involved in; Melanie is engaged in practice as well as in theory with Nussbaum's questions about social justice and capabilities.

The history professor André Wessels, whose name I was given by the archives woman who thought that I was somebody else, replied to my email and said he could spare me just a few minutes. He then generously spared me considerably more than that, gave me copies of his two books on the Anglo-Boer War, and provided a detailed deconstruction of the ongoing debate about what the war should be called: 'Anglo-Boer' versus 'South African'. At the end of our talk he gave me contact details for the curators of the two museums in Simon's Town, where in 1900 Mary Kingsley, the putative third subject of my imagined book, nursed typhoid-stricken Boer POWs in the Palace Barracks Hospital.

24 May
Cape Town. A flying visit only, staying in a guest house in leafy Rondebosch on the lower edge of the University of Cape Town (UCT) campus. This whole area of land once belonged to Cecil

Rhodes. Rondebosch is full of solid, white-painted houses with Dutch gables and sea-green corrugated-iron or tiled roofs, all set in gorgeous gardens behind brilliant blue plumbago hedges. We found the Woolsack, built by Rhodes as an artist's residence for Kipling, where Rudyard, Carrie and their children stayed every year from 1901 to 1908, and peered at it through a locked gate. It is now a postgraduate residence.

Ignoring the advice of every single white person we had spoken to, all of whom insisted, 'You *have* to rent a car in Cape Town', we travelled to Simon's Town by train. The final section of the line, from Fish Hoek to Simon's Town, was opened by Cecil Rhodes with great fanfare in 1890. Now we found the train windows grimy and broken, the seats slashed, the sides of the carriages (inside and out) covered in graffiti. We felt slightly nerve-racked. But it was glorious to be rushing along by the edge of the deep blue sea, stopping at wooden platforms at little seaside towns, where brightly painted houses hug the shoreline below the steep slopes of the fynbos-covered pink-and-green mountains.

In the town museum we found a good collection of photographs of the POW camp at Bellevue on the western edge of town: bell tents; bearded men in shirts, braces and felt hats; preachers; and a number of photos of the prisoners on Windmill Beach, splashing about and bathing under guard and behind barbed wire.

In one of her letters Mary Kingsley described an attempted breakout from the camp – the casualties were brought to the Palace Barracks Hospital. The POWs she was nursing were General Cronjé's surrendered soldiers from the Battle of Paardeberg. They had survived in ditches and tunnels dug into the banks of the Modder River for ten days, alongside the rotting corpses of their friends and their ponies, pinned to their positions by the firestorm unleashed by Lord Kitchener from the other side of the river. By the time they reached the prison ships in Simon's Bay and the POW camp on land, typhoid was rife among them.

When Kingsley contracted typhoid from her Boer patients she knew what it was and what to expect. Her gut became perforated (a common consequence of typhoid); she was operated on, but the strain was too much for her heart. She died in the early hours of Sunday 3 June 1900 (Whit Sunday), and her burial at sea took place the following day, a bank holiday. Main Street, along which her cortège passed on its way to the jetty and the waiting gunboat, was thronged with holidaymakers.

Margaret, the helpful archivist in the Simon's Town Museum, told us how, in 1969 under the government's Group Areas Act, Simon's Town and the other picturesque seaside towns were declared 'whites only' areas and the many 'coloured' (as they were classified under apartheid rule) and black families, some of whom had lived there for generations, were evicted. The coloured families – including Margaret's own – were resettled on the other side of the peninsula at Ocean View (with only a distant view of the ocean); the black families were sent to the dry, sandy wasteland of Gugulethu. Many of the lovely old houses from which families were evicted were left empty and rotting, and were later pulled down. On display in the museum are a good number of old family photographs of those who were driven out. In some cases it seems white rectors and priests closed down their churches and followed their flocks to the townships (that's a euphemism still in use today – 'townships', indeed, as if they are something like Milton Keynes). God, what a ghastly business, and no reparation was ever made when apartheid ended and the ANC came to power. I am amazed by how little bitterness people express when they talk about those times – those quite recent times.

Softly spoken, sandy-haired Commander Steyn of the Naval Museum offered to show us round the Palace Barracks Hospital where Mary Kingsley had worked. He couldn't give us a lift, he explained, because civilians weren't allowed to travel in his special naval car, so we agreed to meet him there. I took poor Mon on a wild goose chase to quite the wrong building; it turned out that the barracks was situated just the other side of the road from the railway station. We had already walked past it once and I had failed to realize what it was. On the way we tried to buy something to eat in the only shop we could find, but promptly stopped trying when we both of us simultaneously spotted a fly creeping out of a hole in the side of a hard-boiled egg that was on display in the food counter. I felt quite sick. Eventually we arrived. The Palace Barracks – so named because it originally belonged to, and was perhaps built by, a wealthy landowner nicknamed 'King John' – is a handsome two-storey building of yellow stone, with two long, flanking wings and steps leading up to a stoep (or balcony) running its whole length. Commander Steyn was already there, patiently awaiting us at the bottom of the steps. It is now where the admiral lives.

When Kingsley stepped away from the wards full of dying men (the hospital was a morgue, she said, rather than a sanatorium), she would sit on the stoep with a mug of Cape wine and some local tobacco rolled into a cigarette, and look out over the bay, where ships crowded with Boer POWs lay at anchor, to where the sun was sinking into the southern ocean.

25 May

We have been out and about in Cape Town with Paula Ensor. Paula was until recently the dean of humanities at UCT; Mon first met her on one of her earlier visits to UFS. She was a student activist in the 1970s, was banned by the apartheid government and went into exile in 1976. Later she was thrown out of the ANC for having 'Trotskyite tendencies'. I really liked her. She took us first to the Vineyard Hotel in Newlands where Rudyard and Carrie Kipling stayed prior to 1900, and then on to the grand Mount Nelson Hotel where they stayed early in 1900 and where Mary Kingsley went to visit them when she arrived in Cape Town. Paula is the only person I have met here who has read (or mentioned reading) my Mozambique book, *S is for Samora*. That is another reason for really liking her.

I have been wondering to what extent the consequences of the Boer War fed into the later consolidation of Afrikaner power and the establishment of apartheid. The war provided a nominal victory for Britain, but self-rule was quickly granted to the beaten Boer Republics and all the promises made by the British to the black South Africans were cast aside. The Boers would become more powerful in the aftermath of the war than they had been before it. The conflict echoes down the years, a piece of the past that still breathes hot on the neck of the present.

Chapter 2

August 2015 – July 2016; Home, London, Home

10 August 2015

Mon and I joined the Labour Party yesterday, and intend to vote for Jeremy Corbyn in the leadership election, thereby joining the ranks of the 'foolish', 'misguided', 'hard left', 'destructive', and so on, according to almost every newspaper pundit on either the right or the left, from *The Torygraph* to *The Guardian*. I haven't seen the *Daily Mail* or *The Sun*; in their pages we are doubtless characterized as swivel-eyed lunatics or even terrorist sympathizers.

12 September

Jeremy Corbyn has become leader of the Labour Party, with 59% of the votes. The Blairites are utterly trounced and furiously angry; they say they can't possibly serve in a Corbyn-led shadow cabinet. I feel it is the most exciting thing that has happened in years.

23 November

On Friday afternoon I met Imogen (Mo) Sutton in Riverstation: £2 for a pot of tea, comfortable sofas, and the most beautiful view over the harbour to the cliffs of Redcliffe and the old harbourmaster's house – which I have always fancied living in – up above them. I told her about the difficulties I was having with the essay on my South African research trip that James McConnachie has commissioned for the Royal Literary Fund (RLF) online magazine, *Collected*. Mo has a helpfully filmic approach, the result of her years of experience storyboarding and then making films with her partner, Richard Williams. She is good at structure.

5 December

I have worked and worked on the South Africa research piece, just an hour or two at a time, trying to be calm about it. It is about the traces of the Boer War in the present-day post-apartheid Free State (what used to be the Orange Free State, one of the Boer Republics with whom Britain went to war); it is also about how I failed to find any traces of the presence there, over 100 years ago, of Rudyard Kipling or of Arthur Conan Doyle. I finished it on Monday and sent it off, and now feel so much better, even though James McConnachie says he won't be able to look at it until after Christmas. In the end, after Mo and I had talked about it, I found a shape for it, a pattern: I have centralized the image of the lonely British military cemetery at Sanna's Post, with its graves and memorials to those who died in the Boer ambush on the last day of March 1900, and have referred to the crash site in the Mbuzini Hills, 500 miles to the east, where Samora Machel and his thirty-four companions lost their lives in 1986. And I have called the piece 'Talking to the Dead', which is what lies at the heart of biographical writing. Now I feel encouraged to write a proposal for the whole book, although in my head it remains nebulous. As a start, I am reading Thomas Pakenham's *The Boer War*. I remember finding his *Scramble for Africa* so useful when I was beginning to think about *S is for Samora*: he presents the close, human detail within a wide historical landscape.

6 December

Anti-Corbyn and anti-left hysteria has been growing ever wilder on the BBC, on ITV, and in *The Guardian*. He has been attacked for voting against us bombing Syria (the UK is now bombing Syria, as if that is a perfectly OK thing to do); he has been attacked for having sixty-six Labour MPs voting with the Tories against him (and had he whipped them into line he would have been attacked for doing that); he has been attacked for appointing a shadow cabinet who don't all agree with each other (yet were they to do so, he would be attacked for appointing only his supporters). Prior to Thursday's Oldham by-election the media were unanimous in forecasting a Labour loss because of the dreaded Corbyn, with Labour votes going to UKIP. When the opposite happened, they all yelped that it had happened *in spite of* the dreaded Corbyn. Was the press as homogenized at the turn of the last century, when we were prosecuting a not-so-small war in a faraway country, as it now appears to be not only in its fear and loathing of Corbyn but in its complacency about bombing Syria?

15 January 2016

James McConnachie made some excellent editorial suggestions on 'Talking to the Dead'; when I had reworked it in the light of his comments, he emailed me to say that I had turned what he thought was a very good piece into a 'sensationally good' piece. How cheering, and how incredibly decent of him. Maybe he says that to everyone, but I don't mind if that's the case; indeed, if so, how thoughtful and generous of him. We all know that's the kind of thing writers want and need to hear, but how many people say it? I wish I could hire him as the editor of my whole (as yet unwritten) book.

6 February

When I got home yesterday I found an email from James McConnachie with the copy-editor's queries on 'Talking to the

Dead'. He (the copy-editor, a fellow RLF Fellow whom I know) had ignored my citations and instead consulted Wikipedia on the subject of the plane crash that killed Samora Machel. Not that Wikipedia is always wrong (far from it, and where would we be without it?), but on contentious issues, such as the history of wars in southern Africa, it is utterly unreliable as the entries are constantly being 're-edited' by people with an agenda (most often a right-wing agenda), as Paul Fauvet and I discovered when we were working together on the Wiki entry for Samora. I spent an hour refuting the copy-editor's changes; the email he sent in response was distinctly shirty.

15 February
My 'Talking to the Dead' essay appeared on the *Collected* website this morning.

12 March
My friend Sara Davies, whom I met soon after we moved to Bristol, has given me an introduction to a literary agent. Back then in 1986, Sara was running the talks and events programme at the Watershed. She had invited Andrea Dworkin, whom we published at The Women's Press, to speak there, and I rang up to tentatively ask if I could come along to say a quick hello to her, explaining that I couldn't come to the actual event as I had a small baby and knew nobody with whom I could leave her. Before I knew what was happening, Sara had arranged for one of her colleagues at the Watershed to look after the baby and I was onstage myself, interviewing Andrea.

Sara told me she thought that this particular agent, with a list of Africa-related books, might well be interested in taking on mine. And she is: not just interested, but hugely enthusiastic, and would like to represent me. This all came about in a phone call on Monday morning. I can hardly believe it. No one has been 'thrilled' or 'delighted' with my work since God knows when. I now have to write a couple of chapters for her to submit and see if she can get it commissioned. To be writing a book that is actually commissioned by a real live publisher! That would be a first for me.

2 April

Yesterday I sent corrected proofs of my ghost story, 'Fran's Nan's Story' (in which a North Somerset farmer is lured into a rhyne by the ghost of a dog that has drowned), to Brian J. Showers of Swan River Press in Dublin for his anthology *Uncertainties*. Later yesterday afternoon C. told me that the very farmer on whom I had based my fictional one and sent to a watery death, the man who owns the field next to our house and who had rudely refused to pay for his share of a new water pipe, had suddenly died. 'Watch out! I might put you in my next novel' was on a T-shirt worn by one of my co-Fellows at an RLF training day a couple of years ago.

8 April

I have just returned from three days in the British Library. As I was hanging around outside the Manuscripts Reading Room on Monday morning, waiting for it to open, two identical-looking middle-aged women came up the stairs towards me, both dressed in fluffy pink polo-neck sweaters and brown slacks. Speaking in strong American Midwest accents, they told me I looked like the woman in the portrait hanging on the wall just behind me. It is Nick Lord's glorious portrait of Hilary Mantel in a jacket of midnight blue and a long scarf patterned in gold and black. She is holding a pen in her raised right hand and has something of the air of a sixteenth-century monarch, appearing simultaneously decorative and authoritative. I said, 'Thank you very much.'

Once inside Manuscripts, I spent the day reading Arthur Conan Doyle's letters, which he wrote in a lovely clear copperplate:

how unlike my dear Rose Macaulay, whose close-to-illegible handwriting was exacerbated by her own idiosyncratic form of shorthand. I read about the family rows over Arthur's inamorata Jean Leckie, just after he returned from the war in South Africa: how he would arrange little holidays with his 'dearest Mam', and she – the mam, complicit in his affair – would invite Jean, who was sixteen years Arthur's junior, to join them as *her* companion. Meanwhile, back in the great big family pile in Surrey, Arthur's wife Touie (Louise), mother of their two young children, was dying of consumption. I didn't find many letters from South Africa, nor any sign of a 1900 diary, which is a disappointment. Doyle's other diaries were redacted by Jean after his death. He was able to marry her in 1907, after long-suffering Touie eventually died. To what extent, I wonder, did being caught between two women (he was too honourable to have abandoned Touie) propel him towards the all-male scenario of the war in South Africa? (I have discovered that, in fact, during the early months of the war South Africa was a bit of a fashionable watering place for upper-class women and their entourages; Winston Churchill's aunt, Lady Sarah Somebody, had a high old time brandishing a rifle during the siege of Mafeking.)

I spent all of Tuesday reading Rudyard Kipling's own run of copies of the Bloemfontein *Friend*, printed on huge broadsheets now browned and brittle. Kipling worked as co-editor of *The Friend* for two or three weeks in March 1900, after Bloemfontein had fallen to the British Army and the newspaper was requisitioned. Its purposes were to boost the troops' morale, to propagandize to the Boers, and to publish new martial laws. Kipling hadn't worked as a jobbing journalist for a good ten years, not since he had left India, and he had a marvellous time, writing later on to one of his co-editors that they would never again enjoy 'such fine Larqs'. The troops were invited to submit poems, jokes and riddles. Kipling himself contributed a series of 'Kopje-Book Maxims' along the lines of 'Raise your hat to the Boer – and you'll get shot', and oversaw a correspondence on whether 'Beards Should be Worn in War'. On the back page they printed notices of horses and ponies lost or suspected stolen, so many of them that it suggests no one took much notice of an edict from Lord Roberts, prominent on the front page, that anyone found in possession of stolen horses would be shot.

On Wednesday I moved downstairs from Manuscripts into Rare Books, where I read a wonderfully lively memoir of the war by an anti-imperialist Belgian nurse called Alice Bron. She went out to South Africa with the international Red Cross to nurse the Boer wounded, but underwent a profound disillusionment with them. She retained her passionate anti-imperialism but ended up nursing the British, whom she found altogether more charming, polite and handsome. I also read a memoir by Erskine Childers, author of *The Riddle of the Sands* and much later shot as a traitor in the Irish Civil War, who looked after the horses belonging to the City Imperial Volunteers (CIV).

Back upstairs in Manuscripts, I saw the identical twins and exchanged a quick whispered greeting. They were sitting at desks facing each other; one was reading a tome on international law, the other a manuscript volume on the French Revolution.

12 April

Today I wrote my first 1,000 words: about what Conan Doyle was up to in October 1899, the month that war was declared against the Boer Republics. I had decided yesterday that I absolutely must make a start; otherwise I could go on forever reading and making notes on my reading. Immediately I became stuck in a sticky bog about how to describe the beginning of the Boer War, and then realized that the only way to do it is to write about the *people*. Of course. I read a really good example of how to write about historical events in the most recent *London Review of Books (LRB)*: Colm Tóibín on the Easter Rising. He starts with Henry James visiting Millbank Prison where various Irish revolutionaries were incarcerated in the 1870s and 1880s, follows them on their release to America, then gives us Conrad and *The Secret Agent*, then Pearse, Joyce, Parnell, Pearse again. From one person to another, and see how history unfolds through their lives. And I have suddenly thought of another master of narrative history: Adam Hochschild, and in particular his account of the struggle to abolish slavery, *Bury the Chains*, which I read a few years ago. It too recreates the past through the lives of a handful of connected individuals.

Conan Doyle was raring to go to the war. He was convinced that the British were fighting for Fair Play: fair play for the 'Uitlanders', the foreigners (many of them British) who had flooded into the Transvaal to make their fortunes from Rand gold, and who were being denied a political voice by the wicked Boers. The Boers' demand for a certain length of residence on the part of these incomers before they could acquire voting rights was seen by Doyle as utterly unreasonable.

Doyle's mother, his 'dearest Mam', had quite a different attitude. She believed we were sisters and brothers under the skin with the Boers, that they were a brave people who had every right to make their own laws on their own land, and that Britain was a nasty bully determined to get its hands on the Transvaal gold and using this business about the Uitlanders' political rights as an excuse. She was far from alone in this view.

Arthur and his mother, Mary Doyle, doted on each other. By now, aged forty and a famous writer, he was de facto head of the Doyle clan, a position he had assumed even while his father was still alive. Alongside her political objections to the war, Mary was terrified that if her son signed up he would become an immediate target for Boer snipers. At sixteen stone (and sporting a fine moustache), Arthur would indeed present a nice target. (One of the things that Alice Bron objected to about the Boers was the pleasure they took in picking off individual specimens from the other side; especially the ones whose medals glinted in the sun.) Fortunately for all the family – he was the eldest of six surviving siblings – Conan Doyle's attempts to enlist were foiled. The Army considered him too old (and possibly too large).

Doyle construed the war in South Africa as a matter of honour. He felt an obligation. He had given up practising medicine some years earlier when the success of Sherlock Holmes had allowed him to become a full-time writer, but he hadn't lost his interest in medical matters. Come December, a few enquiries were made and telegrams exchanged and he was Dr Conan Doyle once more, attached to Langman's private field hospital as a physician and preparing to sail for South Africa in the new year.

The 'dearest Mam' was mollified. Doyle was a little disappointed, but at least he would be near the field of action. Neither of them had any idea that Boer bullets would be a mere bagatelle compared to the war's greatest, and ugliest, killer: typhoid. And in Bloemfontein he would be in the very thick of it.

28 April

The Hillsborough inquests came to an end on Tuesday and the jury brought in a verdict of unlawful killing of all ninety-six who died. At last: after twenty-seven years of struggle. The chief constable, Wright, died in 2011, but all the other culpable, lying police officers are still around. They – the South Yorkshire force – spent over £19 million of public money on lawyers to repeat their lies at the inquests. Yesterday one – just one! – policeman was suspended.

17 June

Jo Cox, Labour MP, aged forty-one and the mother of two small children, was stabbed and shot yesterday lunchtime on her way into a meeting with constituents in the library of her home town of Birstall in West Yorkshire. She died almost immediately. She sounds like an amazing woman: committed, clever and funny; caring about women, poverty and refugees; helping with her local children's hospice; demanding aid for civilians being bombed in Syria. She had been an MP for only a year, and gave a brilliant maiden speech about the diversity and unity in her constituency. Before that she worked on maternal mortality with Oxfam and UNICEF in Darfur. When I heard that she had been shot – they didn't announce that she had died until some hours later – by a fifty-two-year-old man, I thought, Oh my God, she's been shot because she is a woman. But no: it seems she was shot because she was left wing, campaigned for us to stay in Europe, and wanted to help refugees. (Probably also because she was a woman.)

23 June
Referendum day.

26 June
Of those who voted, 48% voted to remain in Europe and 52% to leave. So we are withdrawing from Europe. What a catastrophe. I feel shocked and upset. Nobody knows how it's going to change things, and the demagogues who urge us to leave have no plans for the future. Those who voted leave (some of them, anyway) believe it will make their lives better, more prosperous, but surely it can only make everything worse. David Cameron has resigned.

1 July
I first noticed a month or so ago how debilitating the pain in my shoulders was as I tried to tack up the ponies for our weekly session for the Riding for the Disabled Association (RDA). I usually lead

the pony rather than walk alongside the rider, and I am also one of the tacking-up volunteers. I noticed I could hardly lift up the saddle to place it over Bonnie's back. Saddles are heavy, and at first I thought it was just that I was noticing their weight more, that perhaps it was something to do with getting older, but as each week the pain worsened, I began to have to ask Nicky and Hilary – the two other volunteers on tacking-up duty – for help. As for leading Bonnie, she's one of the easier ones to lead; she's ideal, in fact, as you don't have to drag her along behind you like an overstuffed sofa, nor do you have to haul her in to stop her dashing ahead. But it has still been agony.

At the same time, I have been noticing how hard it is to move my head while I'm driving – not just to look behind me while reversing out of the car park, but even to look to right and left before I swing out into the lane. The dog pulling on the end of her lead is agony in my shoulders; I am regretting never having taught her how to walk to heel. Too late now.

2 July

Terry Pratchett's *Jingo*, which I have been rereading, is all about xenophobia being whipped up and leading everyone to war. The Boer War turned Kipling from an imperialist into a jingoist; by the end of the war his jingoistic zeal outstripped popular opinion. Popular jingoism had reached its apogee with the Relief of Mafeking (celebrated by Kipling in the English South Coast village in which he was then living), and that was during the first year of the war, in May 1900. Pratchett is always so sharp: in *Jingo* he is sharp on how easy it is to stir up fear and hatred of what's not familiar. It is weirdly, unnervingly relevant to what is happening now in Britain. In the last ten days, since the referendum, racists have been given licence to shout abuse at and to physically attack anyone who looks or sounds a little bit foreign. Yesterday I read Alexei Sayle's memoir of growing up communist (*Stalin Ate My Homework*), which Mon gave me; it is full of love for his parents and humour about their membership of the Communist Party, and, like Terry Pratchett's books, is an antidote to these hate-filled, xenophobic days.

7 July

The Chilcot Report on the invasion of Iraq was published yesterday. Tony Blair was wringing his hands all over the place and saying he only did what he thought was right and no one will know how deeply he feels the pain of the unforeseen consequences. Although, as with the Iraq War, many people in Britain saw the Anglo-Boer War as an unprovoked invasion of another sovereign country (or countries), I don't think there was ever an enquiry into its beginnings. In those days it was gold we were after; now it is oil. Back then there were various powerful people hell-bent on having a war, and they drew on writers (notably Kipling) to support them. *Plus ça change…*

We don't read Kipling now for his political views. Why, then, do we (I) read him? For the way he writes of loss and grief, not in their generality but in heart-stopping particularity; for the way his young characters – Mowgli, Kim, Taffy, Stalky – inhabit that tender place that once existed in all of us between innocence and experience; for the way his animals live on the page; for the intricacy of his rhythms and rhymes, the way that his poems, as Mary Kingsley put it (and she was certainly no fan of his political views), 'sing'.

13 July

I have been wondering if I have somehow damaged my shoulder muscles by struggling with the ponies' saddles. This afternoon, with only two or three weeks of this term's RDA left to go, I told Nicky and Hilary that I just can't manage it any longer. And, feeling both feeble and embarrassed, I told the instructor that I don't think it safe for the riders to have me leading a pony. Naturally, everyone was sympathetic, but I feel I have let them down. And I am going to miss the ponies and the kids and the perspective they give me on my own life.

It is as if I am wearing a jacket of burning metal. Or perhaps not so much wearing it, but as if it is fused across my upper back, as if I'm a cyborg. Or as if I have a massive bird of prey sitting on my shoulders, clawing deep into my muscle and bone. I am hunched beneath the pain.

14 July

Last night I crept to a Constituency Labour Party (CLP) meeting at the Ring o' Bells in Nailsea. After a robust exchange of views between the 100 or more members present – it's a long time since I've seen so many elderly men in shirts and braces – we agreed that 'This CLP wishes the Party to unify behind its leader and focus on the political battle with the Tories and stop the internal feuding.' I would say that pro-Corbyn feeling was at about 80% – he is the elected leader, after all – and Corbyn as 'decent fellow but unable to lead the party' at about 20%. There were lots of new members: young women and men, and a surprising number of middle-aged women. Why surprising? Perhaps I've been brainwashed into thinking that middle-aged women all vote Tory.

Chapter 3

July – October 2016;
Oxford, Home, Dublin, Preston, Home

23 July 2016

Oxford. When I arrived on Thursday morning I went straight to the Weston Library in the new Bodleian building, where I had asked Colin Harris, superintendent of the Special Collections Reading Rooms, to order up for me Mary Kingsley's letters to Major Matthew Nathan. Kingsley was thirty-six when she met Nathan at a dinner party early in 1899, just after the publication of her *West African Studies*. He was nine months older than her, handsome, charming, Jewish, and lived with his widowed mother. He was secretary to the Colonial Defence Committee, and, when Mary met him, had just been approached, a day or two earlier, by Colonial Secretary Joseph Chamberlain and asked to go out as acting governor to Sierra Leone in the wake of the Hut Tax debacle.

I was the only person requesting a Bodleian Reader card. The young woman behind the desk was running through the various things to which my three-day card would or would not give me access when suddenly her eye fell on my Bristol University card and she stopped and said, 'Oh, but you're staff!'

'No,' I said, 'not here at Oxford.'

She said, '"Staff" means at any UK university. You get a gold card, and it lasts for four years.'

Feeling very grand, I made my way up to the Mackerras Reading Room on the first floor, flashed my gold card, and found Mary Kingsley's letters to Matthew Nathan awaiting me: a volume bound in green and gold, with marbled endpapers. I thought that perhaps the library had had the letters bound, but no: I discovered from a typewritten commentary, made many years later by a friend of Nathan's called Sir Robert de Zouche Hall, that Nathan himself had had it done. Because he realized that they were important? Apparently throughout his long political career he was a great receiver of women's confidences, and indeed of letters from his female fans; Kingsley was one of only two of his female correspondents to be honoured in this way.

Kingsley published two books on West Africa: *Travels in West Africa* and *West African Studies*. In the former she uses an immediate, self-aware, epistolary tone that sounds curiously modern. It was extremely popular. In the latter she engages more formally with the relationship between colonized and colonizer, and examines some of the often-unforeseen effects on indigenous cultures of colonial rule.

Her letters are closely argued, passionate, witty and self-deprecating. They are much concerned with West Africa – she was politically opposed to the colonial government's imposition of the Hut Tax in Sierra Leone – but they are also deeply personal. One letter, dated 12 March 1899, much quoted by her previous biographers, is twenty-four pages long. In it she talks about her lonely childhood and young womanhood and her sense of alienation from ordinary human society. 'I am no more a human being than a gale of wind is,' she claimed dramatically. In fact she was a skilled raconteur, and was loved and admired by a wide group of friends.

At 2pm I left the library and dragged my suitcase over the road to Wadham College, where I had booked myself in for two nights, and then dragged it, with aching shoulders, to a ground-floor room at the far end of the college. It was very hot inside the room, and I thought at first that the radiators must be on, but they weren't. One of the two windows opened directly onto the street outside; the other onto a sort of wide, dark tunnel, leading to gates onto another street. My first thought: An ideal hiding spot for any lurking burglar or axe murderer. At least there was a standing fan in the room. A previous lodger must have complained of the heat, and of the impossibility of leaving either window open.

I dropped my suitcase and hurried back to the Mackerras Reading Room. Before settling down with the letters, I took a swift lift up to the David Reading Room on the fifth floor, where the Africa material from the old Rhodes House Library is now kept, and where the senior archivist had pre-ordered some stuff for me, to tell them I had arrived and would be up to look at it the following day. Then I went back downstairs and read Zouche Hall's commentary on the letters. It consists of about sixteen flimsies in faint typescript, in which he discusses Mary Kingsley's first biographer, Stephen Gwynn's, use of the letters in his biography, and defends Nathan from the various people who suggested he was exploiting Kingsley's knowledge of West Africa for his own ends.

For supper I had a pint of beer and a dish of whitebait in The King's Arms, over the road from the Bodleian on the corner of Broad Street, and just a step or two from the entrance to Wadham, to whom the pub building belongs. Broad Street is very pretty, I must say. Prettier than Cambridge, but just as full of trampling hordes of tourists. After supper it was too hot to sit in my college bedroom; instead I sat on a bench in a wisteria-dripping courtyard through an archway, and read a few chapters of Justin Cronin's third volume, *The City of Mirrors*, which is not as mind-blowing as his first one, *The Passage*, but has definitely picked up speed from the disappointing second volume *The Twelve*. I had to leave the fan on in my room all night long, or I would have drowned in a pool of sweat.

The next morning the cleaner told me that my room was situated directly over the college boiler, and that was why it was so hellishly hot. She went on to tell me that poor Erin, the undergraduate who had this room last year, had indeed been burgled through the window that leads into the sort of tunnel. I reckon £58 is a bit steep for a room that's too hot to sleep in and offers an open invitation to passing burglars (not to mention axe murderers); surely the college should not put women undergraduates in such an unsafe room.

In the Mackerras Reading Room, Colin Harris kindly showed me the hard-copy catalogue for the Nathan Papers, the details of which I had failed to access online. I find some of these online catalogues quite difficult to navigate. Then I ordered up Nathan's diaries and notebooks, and while I was waiting for them I took the lift upstairs to the David Reading Room. I walked towards the librarians' desk at the far end, and then fell back in astonishment. There, installed behind the desk, magically transported from the lower level, was Colin Harris. He grinned and said, 'Meet the identical twin brother.' The secret staff lift must move even faster than the public lift.

I had pre-ordered various letters, including one from Mary Kingsley in Simon's Town to Flora Shaw, the vigorously imperialist colonial editor of *The Times*, no friend of Kingsley's (but a friend of Kipling's), and found it was just a fragment of a letter, the first page only. Kingsley described the appalling conditions in the Palace Barracks Hospital, to which she had been posted to nurse Boer POWs, and the tiresome interference of a certain Lady Briggs. I am slowly getting used to Kingsley's hand: the wild 'r's and 'p's, and the 't's whose crosses appear three or four letters later, or sometimes stretched out above the word that follows. She punctuates with dashes – or perhaps they are elongated, hurried full stops. There was one word I couldn't make out, so I took the page up to the desk and asked Colin if he was any good at deciphering handwriting. 'That's what archivists do,' he said, 'and I'm only a librarian – but let's have a look.' I had thought the word was either 'wailing' or 'ranting'. Colin glanced at it. 'Writing,' he said at once. Of course. 'Lady Briggs writing to people left and right...' (I guess ranting would also have made sense – or indeed wailing.) The cross of the 't' in 'writing' had slid sideways and was stretched out above 'people'.

I then tried to track down the Holt Papers so as to look at Box 16, which, according to Katherine Frank, Dea Birkett and other biographers of Kingsley (although not her first biographer, Stephen Gwynn, who didn't give references), contains correspondence between Kingsley and John Holt, one of the Liverpool merchants and traders with West Africa, and someone to whom she grew very close. Last week one of the archivists had sent me an internet link to the catalogue but I had failed to find this particular box. She'd told me that there was a hard-copy catalogue too. By now Colin – or his identical twin – had vanished, and the new man behind the desk wasn't nearly as helpful. He sent me down to the mezzanine with a shelf mark that I couldn't find, and then wouldn't respond to my questions about the whereabouts of a hard-copy catalogue. I tried again later, this time with a young woman who looked at the shelf mark I had been given and said, 'That's not kept on the mezzanine, that's why you didn't find it.'

I pressed her about the hard-copy catalogue.

'Well, have you looked over there?' she asked, waving her hand towards the far right-hand corner of the room.

No, of course I hadn't. Why should I have? She led me over, and there on a shelf was the hard-copy catalogue for the Holt Papers. I ordered up (presumably not from the mezzanine but from some other place) Box 16 for the next day.

Back down to the Mackerras to look at Nathan's diaries and notebooks. At the back of one of his small pocketbooks I found a pencil-written draft of a letter to Mary Kingsley. It seems to be a reply to her second letter (I think) to him, in which she begs for understanding of her views on West Africa. 'I do want to understand you and I shall,' he writes in his tiny, neat hand in the pocketbook draft. 'That I do not yet do so at all completely with regard to WA is due to the fact that when I saw you first my interest in that part of the world had not received the stimulus which has j̶u̶s̶t̶ since come to it and if you will forgive my saying so it was your personality rather than your work which engaged my attention at the dinner where we met.' Flirting! And fibbing, too! I am pretty sure that when he met her at that dinner party he had already been unofficially approached about going out to Sierra Leone – I must check that.

In the back pages of his 1899 diary, where he listed letters received, letters written, calls made and dinner parties attended, I saw Nathan had recorded his receipt of Mary's letter of 12 March. Next to it he wrote in brackets, 'her open soul'. According to her previous biographers, he never replied to that letter.

I know already from Katherine Frank's biography that before she left for South Africa and the Boer War in March 1900, Kingsley asked Nathan to come and say goodbye. She told him that on the eve of her departure she would wait in for him in her Kensington house, and that she very much hoped to see him. He did not come, choosing instead to spend the evening at home with his mother. I really do not like him. He exploited her deep knowledge of West Africa for his own ends, while protecting himself, with his privilege and entitlement, not just from an emotional engagement but from any reciprocity. All the smart dinner parties he attended, noted carefully in his diaries! The informal networking between men in positions of power as they passed the port around the table!

A patriarchal world from which Mary Kingsley was, necessarily, excluded.

As I was returning some of the Nathan boxes to the desk I had a very peculiar encounter – or, rather, non-encounter. On the other side of the reading room I spotted a woman whom I instantly recognized as one of our authors from The Women's Press, but I couldn't put a name to her. As I stood in line at the desk I racked my brains for her name but came up only with the title of one of her books. I remembered that the last time I saw her was at the funeral of Ros de Lanerolle, MD at The Women's Press and a very good friend to me, back in the early 1990s. I started to go through the alphabet (as I do with crossword clues), and when I got to 'M' her name revealed itself. At that moment, while I was still standing in line with my Nathan boxes, she came out of the reading area behind me and walked past me to the end of the desk, where she asked one of the librarians for her card, took it, turned, and came back towards me. I was almost directly in her path, and as she approached I greeted her by name, quietly (it being a library) but clearly. She didn't raise her eyes to mine, but muttered in reply either 'Hello' or possibly 'Yes, hello.' It happened so quickly I can't quite remember exactly what she said, and then she scuttled – no other word for it – past me, with her head turned away, and then she was out of the doors and gone. If she had recognized me then she had totally snubbed me. Perhaps she hadn't recognized me, but if so, why had she scuttled off like that, as if she was… I don't know… scared? The whole encounter was utterly peculiar and disturbing. And I was sorry too, because as soon as I had identified her I'd been imagining us catching up on twenty-five years of feminist gossip over a drink that evening. Maybe, when she saw me, she had imagined that too, and had found the prospect unappealing.

So, another evening alone. I returned to The King's Arms and sat at a pavement table and eavesdropped on a twenty-six-year-old doctor explaining to his girlfriend why he probably wouldn't be voting for Jeremy Corbyn again. Then I went back to the bench in the courtyard next to my inferno of a room and carried on with *The City of Mirrors*. Oh, the consolation of fantasy novels!

I had been told that on Saturday the Holt Papers box I had ordered would be delivered to the David Reading Room by 11am, but there was no sign of it when I turned up there. Two librarians were on duty: a woman and a man. The man offered to ring down to the stacks, but didn't seem to know where to find the telephone numbers. The woman handed over a list and he tried two numbers. 'No answer. I could go down to Level 1 and see if it's been delivered there,' he said uncertainly.

I urged him to do so.

Twenty minutes later he returned and said no, and the request slips weren't there either.

I had no idea what that signified: a good thing, or a bad thing? 'Perhaps you could try ringing again?'

He looked alarmed, but did what I suggested. I wondered if perhaps this was his first day in the library.

Then his colleague turned to him and said, 'They listen to music through their earphones down in the stacks. They won't hear the phone ringing.'

I sat myself as close to the desk as I could so that they wouldn't forget me, and started going through my notes from the previous day. Just before twelve I heard a distant rumbling. A minute or two later a young man with thick auburn curls, who looked as if he had been not only listening to music but also smoking a few spliffs, trundled a trolley out from the secret door behind the librarians' desk. And there, at last, was Box 16 of the Holt Papers, a metal box containing a stack of cardboard folders. These held Mary Kingsley's letters to John Holt about West Africa, and letters about her death, including one from the medical officer in Simon's

Town who performed the operation on her perforated bowel. Also present were some letters to Holt from Alice Stopford Green, Irish nationalist, historian, and Kingsley's great friend in the last two or three years of her life, written soon after Mary's death. In one of them Green says that she had always disliked the bonnet Mary wore in her studio portrait because it was so untrue to her (I think she must mean the bonnet with the spray of beads – like an insect's antennae, as Katherine Frank puts it – rather than her workaday sealskin bonnet). In another letter Green says what a traitor Matthew Nathan was ('I grieve to say I look on Major Nathan with much distrust'), telling Holt she had heard that Nathan was going around London dinner parties trashing Kingsley ('now he loses no opportunity of belittling her') and making out she had known nothing about Africa.

27 July

I know I have a tendency to agree with the views of whoever it is I'm reading or listening to (up to a point), so reading Katherine Frank's biography of Mary Kingsley and reading Alice Stopford Green's letters, I'm thinking that, yes, perhaps Kingsley *was* in love with Matthew Nathan (ASG doesn't actually say that, but then she wouldn't, or not to John Holt anyway), and that's why she opened her soul to him, and when her love wasn't requited she went off to her death in South Africa. Frank argues the case convincingly. And I think what an opportunistic bastard Nathan was. He exploited Kingsley's connections, drew on her expertise and then disparaged her when she was dead.

Zouche Hall claims such accusations are nonsense, and that Nathan always spoke highly of Kingsley (though Zouche Hall only mentions in evidence an address to the African Society, nothing else, and as the society was set up in honour of Kingsley it must have been obligatory to praise her); that Nathan had Kingsley's letters bound – an honour extended to only one other of his numerous female correspondents (but might that not have been with an eye to his own honour and standing?); and that a mutual friend of Zouche Hall's and Nathan's, a vicar, had told him that Nathan viewed Kingsley as a good friend (hmm, pretty anecdotal). And why would Alice Stopford Green say that she had heard that Nathan was trashing Kingsley's reputation if she *hadn't* heard it?

Can one state that Kingsley was in love with Nathan unless she says so, admits it, herself? Or at least hints at it? The lonely misery of her last night alone in London is, I think, speculative on Katherine Frank's part. And the letter, the 12 March 1899 letter... yes, it does show her 'open soul', but only to a certain extent. And is she really offering it – the open soul – to Nathan? The letter is, I believe, a master- or mistress-piece of self-construction. Oh, I am becoming a great admirer of clever Mary Kingsley. Nathan didn't appreciate her, or not until long after she was dead, when, thinking of how well it would reflect on him (pure speculation on my part!), he had her letters to him bound up in a beautiful green-and-gold calfskin volume. What a creep!

5 August

A week ago, after my return from Oxford, as I was taking the dog across a field, I found myself in such pain that I burst into tears. I thought, Perhaps after all I *should* go to a GP. Why hadn't I been earlier? Because everyone knows that there is absolutely nothing to be done about back pain except take painkillers, so what was the point?

I rang for an appointment and was told that the earliest one, in three days' time, was with Dr Powell, and would that be all right? Sure, fine, whatever. By the time I got there, I had been crying or on the verge of crying for nearly a week, as I told him when I was called in and found not the Welshman I was expecting, but an extraordinarily tall and handsome Indian-looking doctor in his mid to late thirties, whose name, I realized, I must have misheard; it was probably Dr Pahl. 'Oh, you poor thing,' he said, when I told him why I was there, with such kindness that the tears leapt from my eyes and rolled down my cheeks. He asked me to stand up and he gently touched my shoulders, spine and back, asking where the pain was worst, and whether I could sleep at night, and whether the level of pain was constant throughout the day.

'It eases up in the evenings,' I told him, 'after I've had a glass of wine.'

He laughed. 'There's not much that a glass of wine doesn't help with.'

I felt I could easily fall in love with this man.

'All right,' he said when we were once more sitting down, 'I'd like to send some blood off to be tested as there's a chance – a remote chance – that you might have contracted something called polymyalgia rheumatica. It's not very likely, but just in case...' By then he had the needle ready, and in no time at all the little glass phial was filled with my dark crimson blood.

'This polymy...' I said. 'What is it?'

'Let's see what the blood tests show, and then we can talk about it if necessary,' he said. 'But don't worry, and meanwhile keep taking the paracetamol.'

The next day, when I got home after painfully dragging myself up the lane behind the dog, I heard that the surgery had rung the house. They rang again a couple of hours later, and asked me to make an appointment to go in and see a doctor the following day. I asked if I could see Dr Pahl, but he wasn't in for the rest of the week. What about next week?

'He doesn't seem to be down on the lists for next week, but it would be better if you came in tomorrow anyway, if you possibly can.'

Why the urgency, I wondered? I had been in this state for weeks, and even if it turned out I had contracted the poly-something that handsome Dr Pahl had mentioned, he had told me not to worry.

Those were my last moments of ignorance, not just about polymyalgia rheumatica (or PMR, as its sufferers call it), about which I would come to know a considerable amount over the next months and years, but also about giant cell arteritis, which is associated with PMR in a few – a very few – cases, and which can cause sudden, total and irreversible blindness. My blood – which, as it turned out, was thick with the protein deposits that provide a marker for PMR – turned cold. Irreversible blindness! I took the first appointment available.

12 August

Yesterday I wrote 5,000 words of a rough draft of the second section (Mary Kingsley's travels in West Africa in the 1890s), and today another 1,000 plus, bringing the drafted Kingsley material up to 14,000 words. I am wondering if perhaps the prednisolone – the corticosteroids I have been prescribed to control the PMR – are kicking in? I've been taking 20 milligrams every day since Friday. My elder daughter, HB, tells me that when she was on steroids, just before she went to the Netherlands to take up her postdoc in Groningen with Ben Feringa, she was writing thousands of words every day…

Rather than my shoulders being on fire, I now feel just the shadow of an ache. The GP – not the lovely Dr Pahl, whom I haven't managed to see again – seemed to be saying that the whole point of corticosteroids is that you reduce the dose as fast as you can and then come off them. Or else what? She didn't say. PMR usually 'burns itself out' within six months to a year, she said; and meanwhile I must also take omeprazole daily (to counteract the stomach upset caused by steroids), and alendronic acid in case of the steroids weakening my bones. The alendronic acid I have to take once a week with plenty of water, and then stand upright for half an hour to stop it eating into my stomach. Sounds like an odd kind of medicine – an acid that eats into your stomach – but the GP was insistent.

18 August

Dublin, Grafton Capital Hotel. I am here to read Mary Kingsley's correspondence with Alice Stopford Green at the National Library of Ireland (NLI), and then to attend the Ghost Story Festival, which has been organized by Brian J. Showers, who is the director of Swan River Press, a J. S. Le Fanu scholar, and the editor (with Jim Rockhill) of *Dreams of Shadow and Smoke* (in which appeared 'Alicia Harker's Story', my homage story to Le Fanu's 'Madam Crowl's Ghost') and of the two volumes of *Uncertainties* (my 'Fran's Nan's Story' appears in Volume 1). Lisa Tuttle, who is a guest of honour, will be joining me here. She is on various panels and will be 'in conversation' with two or three of the other attending writers; I am just a punter.

It was a nightmare getting here last night through the pelting rain. The driver of the airport shuttle gave me directions to the hotel when he dropped me off in Kildare Street, but when I got to the corner of St Stephen's Green I lost my nerve and asked a passing woman, who stopped and consulted her phone. As a result I was sent haring off in the wrong direction, my socks already wet through my broken shoes and the hems of my overlarge linen trousers draggling through the puddles. When, oh, when will I learn to use my own phone for directions? Well, not while I am far from home and in a state of panic… The rain fell harder. I was utterly lost. I asked some other people. No one had heard of the Grafton Capital Hotel, nor the street where it was meant to be situated. Thunder overhead, and the skies truly opened. I passed a restaurant full of happy eaters, smugly dry; I turned the door handle and tried to go in but the door was locked. I was nearly crying. Then someone behind the desk keyed me in, and three kind women told me where my hotel was (not far away), and one of them said she would see if they had an umbrella in lost property. They had, and she gave it to me. When I eventually reached the hotel I was soaked through and feeling very sorry for myself. Then I discovered there was no food or drink available. But the girl at reception pointed me to a pub over the road, where I had a pint of beer and a beef sandwich and soon felt much stronger.

This morning I arrived too early for the reader's ticket office at the NLI – back on Kildare Street, hardly any distance at all, as it transpires, from my hotel – so I went down the stairs into the basement to see their W. B. Yeats exhibition. It consisted of recordings of many of his poems, some read by him (a sonorous 'The Lake Isle of Innisfree') and some by others including Seamus Heaney and Sinéad O'Connor, with photographs of wild Irish landscapes. So many famous phrases – just like Shakespeare! 'Pilgrim soul', which both Katherine Frank and Stephen Gwynn (an Irishman himself) use of Mary Kingsley, comes from 'When You Are Old'. Also, through the accompanying exhibition of Yeats's life and times, I discovered that Major John MacBride, a member of the Irish Republican Brotherhood, who married Maud Gonne (to WB's consternation) in 1903, had been in South Africa fighting on the Boer side. The poor chap was executed by the British in 1916.

In the Manuscripts Reading Room, on the second floor in a building a few doors down from the main neoclassical National Library, with dolphins and squirrels and hunting dogs carved around the bases of the pillars that frame the windows, I read Mary Kingsley's letters to Alice Stopford Green, which I had had some difficulty in finding as they are classified as the papers of Mrs J. R. Green, and I hadn't known that Mrs J. R. Green and

Alice Stopford Green were one and the same woman. 'My dear Mrs Green,' writes Kingsley, and then, 'My dear Lady'. Was ASG a lady? Had Mr Green become a sir? No, I don't think so. Mary is funny, gossipy (Alice must have known the Kingsley cousins, Rose and the other Mary, whom my Mary appeared to find such a trial), affectionate, witty, self-deprecating. I am increasingly going off the narrative in which Mary was in love with Matthew Nathan and went off to South Africa broken-hearted. She doesn't sound broken-hearted to me. But what do I know? Mary wrote to Alice that she knew nothing about love; that love, to her, was like ice-capped mountains or glaciers: something you read about rather than experience yourself.

Later, I found out more about Alice Stopford Green. Handsome, red-haired Alice was Irish by birth, and as a young woman moved to London with her sister and widowed mother, where she met the historian J. R. Green and married him. Hence Mrs J. R. Green. He died six years later. Alice became a historian in her own right, and increasingly interested in questions of national independence – especially with regard to Ireland – and British colonialism and imperialism. She would become an important conduit for the afterlife and legacy of Mary Kingsley.

The letters are not in chronological order in the folders; indeed, they are in an awful muddle and one of the two of Mary's letters written from Simon's Town – I think, I'll check again tomorrow – is missing the last page(s). Some of the letters are typed copies, requested by a Dr Gregory in the 1920s, which makes reading ever so much easier. And quicker.

The reading room's main desk provides excellent pencil sharpeners.

A Dr Guillemard was asked by George Macmillan to proofread *Travels in West Africa* to ensure all the scientific bits were correct, and took it upon himself to rewrite Kingsley's text in his own style. It reminds me of the Hurst copy-editor who I thought was checking *S is for Samora* for historical accuracy, but who changed all my verbs and punctuation while failing to pick up on my one egregious error, which was putting Nelson Mandela on Robben Island when he had already been moved to Pollsmoor Prison on the mainland. The mistake was noticed by Zoë Norridge, but she kindly forbore to mention it in her review of the book in *The Independent*. Kingsley wrote Guillemard a wonderfully tactful letter saying that his corrections of style had showed up the overall dreadfulness of her writing, so she was withdrawing the manuscript from him to save him all the trouble and bother.

The library closed at 4.45. On the way (the short way!) back to the hotel, I stopped to watch a dreadlocked street artist performing on a ten-foot-high unicycle at the corner of St Stephen's Green and Grafton Street. He was wearing a military-style jacket and baggy tartan trousers, and had persuaded a woman in the audience to throw three juggling knives up to him, which she did most efficiently. A man who must have been the woman's husband was not happy about this and started an argy-bargy with the juggling unicyclist, but was told to shut up by the rest of the audience.

Lisa arrives tomorrow evening for the Ghost Story Festival and will be sharing my room. In the afternoon I'm taking time out from Alice Stopford Green to go in a minibus organized by Brian Showers to see some mummies in a church crypt.

I'm reading Steve Aylett's weird and funny (when is Steve Aylett *not* weird and funny?) *Lint*, a biography of pulp fiction writer Jeff Lint. Actually, Steve Aylett and Lisa Tuttle are not a million miles apart in their skill with verisimilitude in their weird fictional worlds. I cannot believe that the cult TV cartoon series *Catty and the Major*, which Aylett references frequently in *Lint*, does not really exist. It surely should do! Similarly, when I read Lisa's *My Death* I found the description of Helen Ralston's paintings so convincing that I had to google her to check. I know rationally that both Jeff Lint and Helen Ralston are fictional characters, but I'm not sure I quite believe it.

21 August

The Ghost Story Festival has been terrific, with lots of high-quality panels with speakers coming at the subject – ghost stories, naturally! – in a variety of different ways. David Mitchell was one of the guest speakers. His most recent novel *Slade House* is a ghost story or tale of the uncanny. Brian Showers welcomed me with great warmth, as did the delightful MC John Connolly, who apparently is a hugely famous thriller writer. Usually I feel awkward and out of place at these conventions and festivals, and that I'm there under false pretences, but Brian and John could not have made me feel more welcome.

Yesterday Brian organized a mass signing as so many of the contributors to the *Uncertainties* volumes are here. We all sat at a long table in the main room; rereading my 'Fran's Nan's Story' I reckon it can hold its own with the other stories in the two volumes. Lisa is much looked up to by the younger women writers here, and when someone realized that I was the author of *In the Chinks of the World Machine*, suddenly everyone was acting as if Lisa and I were a pair of elder stateswomen, or possibly even wise old witches.

About twelve of us signed up to go and gawp at the 'mummies'. They turned out to be mummified bodies in the vaults of St Michan's Church, which, as M. R. James says in 'Lost Hearts', his tale of beastly child murder, 'possess the horrid property of preserving corpses from decay for centuries'. From a central corridor or tunnel we looked through an archway into a chamber with bodies laid out on the stone floor: a nun, a man with his right hand and both his feet chopped off, a naked woman. 'Did you touch them?' Brian asked me on our return. No, I had not! Ugh, the very thought!

But it was amazing and weird to be only an inch or two away from them. I could have touched them had I wanted to. The nun's toenails and fingernails looked perfectly preserved.

25 August, or is it 26?
I have been so ill that I have lost track of dates. I must have picked up something in Dublin or on the Ryanair flight home. It has gone to my chest and exacerbated the chronic back and shoulder pain of the polymyalgia. Having dutifully reduced the steroid dose to 15 milligrams, I have put it back up to 20, with no discernible improvement. I was meant to be going to London on Wednesday to meet my new agent – a new agent after being agentless for so many years – but I was incapable of getting even as far as the train station. I was bitterly disappointed. Instead I lay on my sickbed and read John Connolly's first Charlie Parker novel on my Kindle. It is very dark, a little bit supernatural, and utterly gripping.

22 September
Lancashire Infantry Museum, Preston, on a day trip up from staying with Mon in Keele. Half of a battalion of the Loyal (not a mistaken alternative to 'Royal', as I had originally thought) North Lancashire Regiment, under the command of Lieutenant Colonel Robert Kekewich, was in Kimberley – the diamond-mining town on the border of Cape Colony and the Free State – when it came under siege by the Boer forces at the end of 1899. Kekewich – oh, wonderful man – kept a journal of the siege. The museum is housed in the regimental barracks, which were designed by John Chard of the Royal Engineers who, in the war against the Zulus ten years prior to that against the Boers, took over command at Rorke's Drift when the other British officers were killed. He ordered the construction of a defensive wall of biscuit boxes (which in those days were made out of tin), and was awarded the Victoria Cross.

I left the car in a public car park close by the barracks and walked up to the gates. A sign on one of the pillars read, 'Explosive atmosphere.'

'What does that mean?' I asked the official in the gatehouse.

'It means there's an armoury on the premises.' He took all my details, including date of birth, 'in case the armoury blows up and we have to inform your next of kin'. I couldn't tell whether or not he was joking.

The archivist, Jane, led me into a beautiful high-ceilinged room, wallpapered in gold and maroon stripes, with light pouring in from tall windows on either side. Regimental drums were on display against the walls, with ancient tiger skins draped over them and, hanging above them, faded regimental banners. Jane told me they have to be vigilant against moths. She gave me a seat at one end of an immensely long table gleaming with polish, where she had already laid out the typescript copy of the surviving parts of Kekewich's journal. 'Did the regiment use to use this table for their banquets in the nineteenth century?' I asked her.

'Oh no, it's quite a recent acquisition: they brought it back from Nazi HQ in Germany.'

Museums are random memorials to the dead. Kekewich's cufflinks and a few photographs are on show in a glass case at the bottom of the stairs.

Kekewich had the misfortune to have Cecil Rhodes trapped in Kimberley with him during the siege, countermanding his every order and behaving as if he owned the town. Which in a way he did, being a majority shareholder and director of the diamond-mining consortium. Rhodes backed up Kekewich only if he agreed with him but, as Kekewich reported to Lord Roberts, 'he desires to control military situation'.

'I have put up with insults so as not to risk safety of defence,' Kekewich continued. Kekewich himself was mild-mannered, courteous and conscientious, deeply concerned for the lives and welfare of all the civilians trapped in Kimberley. He spent hours every night sending and receiving messages from the British general sent to relieve the siege, who was himself trapped by Boer forces twenty miles away, and every dawn he climbed the conning tower constructed above the huge mining pit. 'I am very short of sleep... My staff too are suffering much for want of sleep,' he wrote at the beginning of one entry. He had to deal with outbreaks of scurvy, with cattle sent out to graze being stolen by the Boers, with lack of food, and when for lack of wood to make fires he reluctantly forbade the boiling of water, which led to the inevitable outbreak of typhoid. The diary is wonderfully vivid.

Two years after the end of the war Kekewich, promoted to full colonel, retired from the Army. He was called back in 1914, aged sixty, and given command of the 13th (Western) Division. Soon afterwards, Jane told me, he shot himself in the head. He had been suffering from insomnia and depression; perhaps it was more than he could bear to witness once more the suffering and trauma of those under his care.

27 September

A blood test shows that my CRP (C-reactive protein, a protein released by the liver that marks inflammation in the body) has risen from 4 (normal) before I went to Dublin, achieved after a month of steroids, to 25. It feels like it. My shoulders and neck are on fire.

29 September

My new agent has told me she hasn't yet read the two chapters that I sent her two and a half weeks ago to add to the one that I sent her earlier, but says she will send me notes on all of them next week. What I need to do is polish these three – the ones that cover the early lives of Kipling, Kingsley and Conan Doyle – along with the proposal, add some illustrations to the text, and then she'll start pitching to publishers in November. 'It would be nice to have a deal before Christmas, wouldn't it?' A deal? Before Christmas? That would be an entirely new – and delightful – experience for me.

12 October

The agent has *not* sent the promised notes on my first chapters. She is now presumably in Frankfurt for the Book Fair and will be caught up with post-Frankfurt business for the next two or three weeks at least. Well, I must just carry on without her response. It would be folly to wait. I shall start thinking about Mary Kingsley in South Africa.

I am so missing RDA: my weekly shot not just of ponies (the sweet grassy smell of them, the warmth and softness of their coats, their velvet noses and huffing breath) but also of the decent, pony-loving, community-minded women who make up the group of volunteers.

Last Tuesday I went up to 25 milligrams of prednisolone, and at last, after seven days, the pain is easing; the burning fire has become a dull ache. I am going to stay on this dosage for a bit despite the GP bleating about diabetes and osteoporosis and blood sugar and God knows what else. Meanwhile a tiny bit of research on my part has revealed that while alendronic acid is just the ticket for binding calcium to your bones if you actually suffer from osteoporosis, it is absolutely not a prophylactic. It does nothing (except burn your stomach and poison you) if you don't have osteoporosis, which I don't. I have stopped taking it.

Oh, for handsome, kindly Dr Pahl! I know that he would be pragmatic about my pain, and wonderfully (handsomely) sympathetic. Over the last couple of months, whenever I have attended the surgery, I have looked for his name and photo on the large noticeboard beside the reception desk, where everyone who works at the surgery in whatever capacity is listed. No sign of him. I have not seen or heard of him since that first appointment. Was he a locum? Maybe. Or maybe not. Perhaps he came from the same place as the tall fair-haired woman in hiking boots who – one afternoon ten years or so ago – emerged out of thick fog and found me in a tearful panic because my aged Border collie Sky had had some kind of seizure and was lying stretched out on his side by the footpath. This warrior woman picked him up and carried him across the bare winter fields to where I had parked the car, laid him on the back seat, then walked off into the fog. I have never set eyes on her again.

Chapter 4

November 2016 – March 2017; Home, London, Home

10 November 2016

Yesterday Donald Trump won the election to be the next – forty-fifth – President of America. Well, he won the electoral college votes and that's what counts; in fact Hillary Clinton won marginally more individual votes.

On BBC One news last night Jon Sopel said that while Trump had been an outsider all along, in his victory speech he was behaving like a 'true statesman'; at which point I turned over to ITV, where Robert Moore was saying how important it is not to normalize Trump and his victory, and to remember that this is the man who has the backing of the Ku Klux Klan, and who is responsible for spreading the lie (among hundreds of other lies) that Barack Obama wasn't born in the USA. Today Trump will meet Obama in the White House, and will begin to dismantle the healthcare insurance for poor people – Obamacare – that Obama has struggled, in the teeth of Republican resistance, to put in place.

Various pundits are on the airwaves saying that this is a vote against globalization and the political elite. Is it? If so, it is surely also a vote, as with Brexit, against foreigners and against the future. Elderly, obese white men voted for Trump because they hate women and hate black people, and they want abortion to be criminalized.

11 November

I received an email from Julia Copus, who was my mentor when I was one of the RLF Writing Fellows at Exeter University, and whom I last saw a few years ago when I went to the launch in Taunton of her poetry collection *The World's Two Smallest Humans*. She is a very nice woman and a fine poet. *TWTSH* contains a wonderful sequence of poems about IVF. She was writing to say that she had bumped into my dear friend Michèle Roberts at the unveiling of a blue plaque at the childhood home of Charlotte Mew in Bloomsbury. Julia is writing a biography of Mew. She said, 'It's a lonely business, isn't it, writing a biography?'

I wonder, is it lonelier than other forms of writing? Than writing fiction, say? Maybe, if you consider the length of time you spend doing it. As if you're in a three- or four-year relationship (or even longer) with a ghost, trying all that time to drag them back from the dead, trying single-handedly to make them live again.

On the other hand – in my case, anyway – I engage in all sorts of conversations (mainly, I admit, conversations inside my own head) with other people who have thought and/or written about my subjects. And when I was working on Rose Macaulay and on Samora Machel I actually met people who had known them. Whereas novelists and poets are always necessarily alone with their own words.

15 November

On 5 November I went down to 22.5 milligrams of prednisolone, and it was fine – i.e. bearable pain in the mornings, and almost pain-free by evening. I started going to tai chi classes again, bolstered each time by two paracetamol. I would have stayed on 22.5 for two weeks, but I ran out of 2.5-milligram pills, so yesterday I reduced further to 20 milligrams. Next week I have an appointment in the rheumatology department in the Bristol Royal Infirmary (BRI).

8 December

Back on 22.5 milligrams of prednisolone and feeling bloated. The rheumatologist suggested that I stay on 22.5 for three weeks, and then reduce by 2.5 every three thereafter. The pain is now not too bad, but oh dear, my face has become round like the full moon and I've developed a double chin. I have also got mouth ulcers.

9 December

This morning I sent off a reworked proposal and the first three redrafted chapters of *Escape to Africa* (Mo Sutton's suggested title) to my agent. These are the chapters on Kingsley, Kipling and Conan Doyle's childhoods. She had asked me to insert pictures into the text, as that would make it more attractive to commissioning editors. (Really? They must be rather shallow editors, I reckon, if they need to be attracted by pictures.) It took me two whole days to transfer the pictures into the text: the text kept on rearranging itself into strange conformations, and I found it difficult to control the size of the pictures. I can't help thinking this is a waste of time. It's not as if I've yet got permission to use these pictures anyway.

13 December

I have been awarded the £3,000 grant I asked for from the Authors' Foundation. How incredibly affirming and encouraging! Michèle, who is on the committee but disclosed her friendship with me and withdrew from the decision-making, emailed me last night to let me know.

14 December

Dad would have turned ninety-seven today. It is a lovely sunny day with a pale blue winter sky; blackbirds are eating the scarlet apples on the leafless branches of the crab apple tree. I am gloriously alone in a quiet house, reading Julia Szołtysek's A *Mosaic of Misunderstanding:*

Occident, Orient and Facets of Mutual Misconstrual, in which she cites not only my *Rose Macaulay* but also my research journal for that biography, *Dreaming of Rose: A Biographer's Journal*.

28 December

No, it wasn't £3,000 from the Authors' Foundation – it was £4,000! How come I was so bold as to ask for £4,000? So bold, and so unlike me, that I actually forgot that that was the amount I asked for. It will make a huge difference – it will cover most of my research expenses, including another trip to South Africa. The cheque arrived the day before Christmas Eve.

2 January 2017

PMR: I reduced to 17.5 milligrams of prednisolone three days ago. The pain is creeping back, a little more severe each day. 20 milligrams appears to be some kind of limit, a dividing line between manageable and debilitating pain.

3 January

On my way by train to London on a cold, bright, frosty morning, to go to the Royal Geographical Society, where I hope to see, among other things, Mary Kingsley's *hat*, the notorious sealskin hat; and then tomorrow to the House of Lords to read her correspondence with her friend John St Loe Strachey, who was editor of *The Spectator*.

The hedges sparkle with frost; their shadows lie long and dark on the ground. What pleasure! Both the going to London and the brightness of the day. I have enjoyed the last week of quiet reading at home, but the early evening countryside darkness is lowering to the spirits, and I'm glad to be away from it and heading towards the lights of the capital.

Later: in the Foyle Reading Room in the basement of the Royal Geographical Society I read Mary Kingsley's four joyful, high-spirited letters to her friend Violet Roy, from on board the SS *Lagos* on her first voyage down the West African coast in 1893. She struggles with an octopus that creeps on board, falls into a cellar in a shop in Sierra Leone as she tries to avoid a dog-faced monkey that has just bitten one of her fellow passengers, and complains about a dour Scotsman who was her designated 'Custodian'. She much prefers the company of the whisky-drinking captain.

In a corner of the reading room stands a wooden fetish statue, a *Mavungu*, from West Africa, very similar to Kingsley's *Mavungu*, which was given to her by a Portuguese trader in Cabinda, and which she set as a guard by the door of her flat in Kensington. Many of the iron nails and other bits of metal have been removed from the face and torso of this one in the RGS: you can see the holes in the wood where they were hammered in. In the *Journal of West African Studies* I found three photographs of Kingsley's *Mavungu* (now apparently in the Pitt Rivers Museum in Oxford): staring-eyed, open-mouthed, its head and torso positively bristling with rusted nails. Mary believed her *Mavungu* retained its ancient powers for it still wore, around its neck, a band of coagulated human blood.

I ordered up Kingsley's moth-eaten hat from the storeroom. Her friends used to describe it as sealskin, but it looks more like moleskin to me (as indeed it is catalogued). The fur has a reddish tinge.

Later I looked at Dea Birkett's useful Kingsley bibliography, and a copy of the second edition of Kingsley's *West African Studies* with only partially cut pages. This edition includes as appendices Kingsley's two public talks on imperialism. One of them was the last talk she ever gave in London, at the Imperial Institute. I hope I might find another copy of this edition in one of the Bristol libraries. I also looked at a bound volume of West Africa pamphlets by authors various, donated by the slippery Matthew Nathan himself.

4 January

House of Lords archives. There is one other researcher here: an elderly man looking at old maps. The only sounds are the rustling of paper as he unfolds and refolds his maps, and the ticking of a wall clock.

Researchers are allowed into the Houses of Parliament an hour before they open to the general public, so when I turned up this morning at the main entrance there was no one else around and I whizzed past the policemen at the gate and down a ramp to the security checkpoint. I had completely forgotten I was carrying a little wooden-handled Choix Opinel knife in my handbag. The man searching my bag found it (of course), took it out, opened and closed the blade, and suddenly, quietly, from I don't know where, the room was full of an awful lot of very large security men; four of them just appeared from a dark doorway that I hadn't even noticed. They positioned themselves, as if casually, on the far side of the desk. Doubtless they would be over it in a flash if they thought it necessary. The first man, the one who had found the knife, said he would have to discuss this with his superior. He walked at a normal pace to the door, and once through it he absolutely hared up the ramp – even faster than I had come down it – to the policemen at the top who had recently waved me in so cheerily. I overheard some low chat among the apparently casual security men about 'intent'. I was nervous, a bit shaky, but tried not to show it. Then the man came back and said, OK, he'd take the knife and give me a receipt for it. He told me that were it a folding knife without a locking collar it would be all right (all right? I surely wouldn't have been allowed to take it inside), but lockable knives are illegal under the

1953 Prevention of Crime Act (I found out later this section was introduced to stop Teddy Boys carrying knives). So not only was I trying to smuggle a knife into the Houses of Parliament, but it was an illegal one. By then a couple of the large men had faded away back to where they had come from; with the remaining ones I exchanged a bit of banter about how dangerous unlockable knives were – in terms of slicing off your thumb while peeling an apple, and so on – as I felt my heart rate begin to slow down towards normal. Then I was sent on my way, with a receipt for a 'wooden handle knife lock'.

In my email exchange with the House of Lords archivist I had been told that I would have to be escorted from the main entrance to and from the archives, via a place called Lower Waiting; in fact I had to find my own way through the Great Hall and up the steps to the Central Lobby, where the man behind the desk said he was new to the job and hadn't ever heard of Lower Waiting. I spotted a security guard lurking nearby: he informed me that Lower Waiting was currently having its floor retiled and was therefore out of bounds, but he personally would escort me to the archives...

First of all he escorted me to the library. A mistake, as one of the librarians pointed out in a chilly manner. Is there bad blood between the library and the archives? Old feuds? We were directed (coldly) to the Victoria Tower, home to the archives. My security guard, who seemed reluctant to release me, brightened up at this news, and promised to take me to the Tower by the 'scenic route'.

Mary Kingsley really liked John St Loe Strachey. He published a number of her letters in *The Spectator* on the subject of the arrogance and folly of the representatives of the Church Missionary Society in West Africa, and the arrogance and folly of the British government in trying to ban the liquor trade. The tone of her letters to him is intimate, trusting, urgent. It is annoying that Stephen Gwynn reproduces the letters in his biography without putting in any ellipses to indicate the cuts that he has made. One of the passages he had cut, I discovered as I read Kingsley's original letter to Strachey, concerns a rumour she heard on board the SS *Moor*, on the way out to Cape Town in March 1900, about a huge cache of soft-nosed or 'dumdum' bullets in Ladysmith. These must be the same kind of bullets that Conan Doyle was puzzling over as he picked his way over the battlefield of Sanna's Post. They were banned from use in the war against the Boers, but before the war were commonly used against the 'natives'; Kingsley tells Strachey that she has heard there were millions of rounds of them at Ladysmith, and that General White didn't have time to destroy them. Therefore, his getting holed up under siege in Ladysmith was a jolly good thing, and possibly even a deliberate move rather than, as most people thought, a cowardly act of folly. The discovery of a cache of banned bullets would have been a propaganda disaster for the British.

I couldn't resist, while I was there, checking to see if Strachey had corresponded with Arthur Conan Doyle and Rudyard Kipling, too. Of course he had! The Kiplings were friends of the Stracheys; they used to go and stay with them in their 'delightfully quaint house' at Merrow Down near Guildford, the inspiration for Kipling's poem 'There runs a road by Merrow Down...', the beautiful, poignant, pain-soaked elegy for his daughter Josephine, who died in 1899 aged six.

I found five or six letters from Conan Doyle. Friendly, courteous ones from the 1900s and 1910s, about interests he and Strachey had in common, such as volunteer and conscription armies, and about Rifle Clubs – Doyle had set one up on his return from South Africa which he called, in his rather ponderously jokey way, the Hindhead Commando of Burghers; then a letter from the early 1920s in which he addresses Strachey as 'Dear Sir', rather than 'Dear Strachey', and goes on to complain bitterly about a review by

Strachey of one of his books on spiritualism. Doyle tells Strachey that spiritualism is the most important thing in the world. Doyle believed spiritualism was his Big Purpose, the reason he had been put on this earth. I suspect he fell out with a good number of his friends over this.

At the end of the day, once I had reclaimed my illegal Choix Opinel from the cupboard where confiscated items are held, I was closely escorted to the exit gates – I suppose in case I suddenly ran amok and stabbed Theresa May.

5 January
Back at the Houses of Parliament this morning, I was greeted in Security with smiles and banter: 'Haven't brought your knife with you today, have you, hurr, hurr?' and so on.

6 January, Feast of the Epiphany
After I left the House of Lords archives yesterday morning I took the tube to High Street Kensington and walked westwards, in search of 32 St Mary Abbots Terrace, the little house Mary Kingsley and her brother Charley moved into in the summer of 1898, and 100 Addison Road, the flat they had lived in before then. I found St Mary Abbots Terrace, running parallel to the High Street on its northern side, but the even numbers, consisting of semi-detached blocks of four, go up only as far as 28. A tall block of flats called Abbots House now stands where I would have expected to find numbers 30, 32, 34 and 36. A private security guard told me the block dates from the 1960s. Perhaps numbers 30 to 36 were bombed during the war? Addison Road starts just around the corner, heading north at right angles to the High Street. I set off to find number 100, where the Kingsley siblings lived in the top flat prior to moving to St Mary Abbots Terrace. The numbering starts at the Kensington end, with large houses standing in their own grounds. I felt as if I had

walked at least a couple of miles, uphill, before I reached the top, northern, Holland Park end, where number 100, a large detached house next door to the pink-fronted Cardinal Vaughan Memorial School, proved to be the very last building. An enormously tall London plane grows right up to the attic windows of number 100: were Mary and her brother living in the attic, or were they on the third floor? By then I was exhausted, so I took a bus along Holland Park Avenue to Holland Park tube station. In Danny Dorling's 2013 book about the people who live along London's Central Line, *The 32 Stops*, he reports that between Shepherd's Bush (one stop to the east) and Holland Park, 'two minutes' tube travel and a single stop, life expectancy rises by seven years'.[4]

I was the only person walking through the tunnel to get to the platform, and once there I was one of only three passengers waiting for a train. I had no idea that any London tube station could ever be so empty on a Friday afternoon. It was unnerving. I am feeling mentally and physically exhausted, and have been sleeping heavily at night through wild and crowded steroid dreams.

On the train back to Bristol I was reading Boris Strugatsky's afterword to the Gollancz 2012 edition (part of their SF Masterworks series) of *Roadside Picnic*, which J gave me for Christmas. The term 'Stalker' in the novel (used by Tarkovsky as the title for his famous 1979 film) was taken by the Strugatsky brothers from Rudyard Kipling's *Stalky & Co*. Years earlier, when he was still a student, Arkady Strugatsky had translated *Stalky & Co* into Russian, and given it the title *Stullky and Company*. 'When we were thinking of the word "stalker", we undoubtedly had in mind the streetwise Stullky, a tough and even ruthless youth, who, however, was by no means without a certain boyish chivalry and generosity.' They said that for years they didn't realize 'Stalky' was pronounced 'staw' rather than 'stull'.

---

4   *The 32 Stops: The Central Line* by Danny Dorling, 2013, Penguin, p. 48.

13 January

Freezing cold, bitter wind, but as yet no snow, although snow is falling both to the east and the west of us.

18 January

For the last few mornings the burning pain in my neck and shoulders has been getting worse. But I *must* reduce the steroid dose. I now have bulging cheeks as well as a double chin, and so many rolls of fat round my waist that the elastic of my tai chi trousers rolls over rather than remaining flat: uncomfortable as well as painfully tight. It's not just my clothes that feel tight: my actual *skin* feels tight.

19 January

I emailed John Walker, the Kipling Society librarian, to ask if he could help me solve the mystery of Kipling's 'three dear ladies' of Kensington, as I had searched everywhere etc., etc. He wrote back politely and referred me to page whatever of Andrew Lycett's biography, where I found that Lycett not only names them but gives lengthy details. I could have sworn I'd read his whole book. If I did, then it was obviously without sufficient attention. One of the dear ladies was a prolific and successful novelist called Georgiana Craik, who was a cousin by marriage of an even more successful novelist called Dinah Craik. It was in their flat that Mary Kingsley and Rudyard Kipling first met, apparently. What was the dear ladies' connection to Kingsley? I'd better read some more biographies – and this time pay more attention to what I am reading!

I have been laboriously captioning and crediting the photos I've taken from inside various books (annoyingly, some come from books I've already taken back to the library without noting the appropriate details). I suddenly realized that I had read only the second half of Harry Ricketts' *The Unforgiving Minute*. I started at the beginning yesterday, and what did I find? The 'three dear ladies' of Kensington named and described. If I ever get to meet John Walker of the Kipling Society I shall be too embarrassed to introduce myself.

Ricketts writes a good preface about Kipling's chameleonic qualities and his various different identities, and notes how Kim and Mowgli, orphans both, pass from one identity to another, never fully belonging. Rudyard and his little sister Trix, cast out by their parents at the ages of five and three, were also, essentially, orphans. 'Little Friend of All the World': that was how Ruddy was known to the adoring Indian servants in Bombay (and the name by which Kim is known in the markets and the streets) before he was exiled to cold, loveless England. *Kim* is a retelling of Kipling's pre-expulsion days, says Ricketts, or a tale of what happens to someone who is *not* expelled.

Ricketts gives a detailed ancestry: Alice Kipling's mother Hannah (Rudyard's grandmother) was Methodist minister George Macdonald's second wife. She gave birth to *eleven* children, seven of whom survived into adulthood.

Those Victorian clergymen: they just couldn't keep their pricks inside their pants. Arthur Conan Doyle's 'dearest Mam' bore and gave birth to nine children over twenty-one years. Her husband Charles Doyle (not in fact a clergyman, but an illustrator) was an alcoholic and intermittent maniac. What a relief it must have been for her when he was finally put away for good.

Harry Ricketts calls George Macdonald 'a cheerful, broad-minded workaholic'. Oh yes? Show me a 'workaholic' and I'll show you a man who has washed his hands of domestic and family life, and prefers to have nothing to do with his wife except when impregnating her, and maybe not much even then. Mary Doyle lost two children in infancy; Hannah Macdonald four. Hannah 'possessed a more troubled temperament than her husband'. Ricketts suggests that her 'melancholy tinge' was religious in nature; I would have thought it was more likely a consequence of obligatory sex, eleven pregnancies, and watching four of your children die, while your husband is busy 'working'.

20 January
In *The Open House*, one of Michael Innes's donnish thrillers (as he actually *was* a don, perhaps it's not surprising that some of his novels are donnish), one of the characters, a professor, says to Sir John Appleby, on hearing that he is a retired policeman, 'I expect you knew my friend Strickland.' Strickland the policeman (and master of disguise) appears only fleetingly in *Kim*; twice, I think: once galloping up the Road and exchanging gossip with the Maharanee in her covered wagon, and again when he appears at Delhi railway station and rescues the secret agent E23. He appears in one or two of Kipling's *Plain Tales* as well, and two or three later stories. Innes's professor says of his friend Strickland, 'Ran your show on the hush-hush side. Keeping an eye on the Tsar and all that.' A couple of pages later Innes nudges his readers further by having the professor refer to Kipling by name: '…used to have long chats about the [Shakespeare] plays with Mr Kipling. Another strong Shakespeare man. Bible too. Amazing.'

The Open House and *Roadside Picnic*, in which the Strugatsky brothers pay homage to Stalky, were both published in 1972. Are Kipling's fictional characters still referenced in genre fiction nowadays, I wonder?

I'm sure a policeman called Strickland makes an appearance in other fiction, too – in *A Dance to the Music of Time*? Or somewhere in Orwell, perhaps?

21 January
Yesterday Donald Trump was sworn in as the forty-fifth President of the United States, despite Hillary Clinton having won nearly three

million more votes than he did. His speech was full of nothing: make America great again, America first; among his cheering audience were people calling out for Clinton to be locked up. His hatred – of women, black people, Mexicans, liberals…well, just about everyone – gives permission to all the sad, lonely, fucked-up gun-owning creeps to express *their* hatred. So, this morning I went on a women's march against Trump, beneath a brilliant blue sky, joining up with Helen Taylor and Pat Ferguson and a group of their friends. 500 or 600 of us marched round Queen Square under banners that read 'Love Trumps Hate', 'Girls Just Wanna Have Fun(damental Human Rights)', 'This Pussy Bites Back', and so on. Then we crossed the Horsefair and headed up the hill to College Green. One woman scattered leaflets with a photo of Trump on them and invited us to trample on him.

I have been reading in the Kipling biographies about Kipling's friendship with Teddy Roosevelt, who would become the twenty-sixth President of the USA. Kipling was full of romantic admiration for Roosevelt's Rough Riders, the volunteer or (hmm) freelance cavalrymen who rode against the Spanish to take Cuba for America. Small, short-sighted, inky-fingered Kipling was always a great admirer of manly men – in the Boer War it was the wild colonial boys: the tall Australians and outdoorsy New Zealanders. I find it rather endearing. He wrote his famous (or infamous) poem 'The White Man's Burden' – what he called his 'poem about expansion' – as a sort of invitation to the USA to join in the imperial endeavour. It was already doing quite well, what with Cuba and the Philippines and Puerto Rico. I find this rather less endearing.

27 January

January always goes on forever. I've heard nothing yet from my agent, whom I emailed a week ago last Monday – that is, nearly a fortnight ago – passing on to her my friend Lara Feigel's generous suggestion that we try the synopsis and early chapters on her (Lara's) editor at Bloomsbury. I met Lara in June 2012 in the Wren Library in Trinity College, Cambridge, on the occasion of the opening of the embargoed box of Rose Macaulay's letters. She was doing research for her book on writers in London during the Blitz, and appears in the pages of my *Dreaming of Rose*.

What do I do now? I feel as if I'm writing into a void. I long to be given direction. Meanwhile I'm rereading Mary Kingsley's racy, stylish *Travels in West Africa* and thinking vague and random thoughts about similarities in style between Kingsley and Macaulay, for the lecture I have been invited to give at the A Suitcase of Her Own: Women and Travel conference organized by Julia Szołtysek at the department of postcolonial studies and travel writing at the University of Silesia in Poland.

1 February

After two weeks of silence from my agent after I had enquired about whether she was planning to submit my proposal and chapters, as she had said she would do first in November and again last month, I received an email from her in Chicago. She had *loved* the proposal, but had been unable to open the file containing the first three chapters (which I sent before Christmas, for Christ's sake) so please would I re-send it?

How fortunate that I was able to overcome my anxiety and unwillingness to chase her about the material I had sent her. Otherwise I might not have heard about this for months. I spent quite some time yesterday trying to send the chapters to her techno-whizz young assistant at the agency. The trouble was caused (I think) by all the pictures I had so painstakingly – and, I suspect, uselessly – inserted into the text. Eventually the techno-whizz managed to open them – text, pictures and all – so maybe when the agent returns next week she'll read the chapters and actually do something.

9 February

My shoulders and spine feel fully inflamed again, as if I am strapped into a burning harness. I'm taking 12.5 milligrams of prednisolone daily; simultaneous with the fiery pain I feel swollen up and like I'm straining against my clothes.

18 February

Paddington station, waiting for the 11am train home. On Wednesday I went to the Natural History Museum (NHM) to look at Mary Kingsley's correspondence with Dr Albert Günther, author of the standard work *An Introduction to the Study of Fishes*, a copy of which she took with her on her West African travels (along with an edition of Horace's *Odes*), and who would become her mentor, then colleague and friend. It was half-term: God, what mayhem. I fought my way through crowds of children, parents, grandparents, nannies, toddlers, and babies in huge buggies, to reach the library doors, through which I fell with utter relief.

I told the librarian that I had found it very difficult to find the Kingsley letters in the online catalogue. She explained that there was no cross-referencing between archives and library catalogues, and that was why it was tricky. In fact it seems impossible to get details out of either of the catalogues. But then, I know that catalogue research is not my forte. I'm always having to ask people for help. In this instance it didn't seem entirely my fault. The librarian said she thought there was a paper catalogue somewhere, and went off to have a look for me. No luck. But instead she returned with a box full of actual, real letters (how on earth had she found them without a catalogue entry?): twenty-five of them, from Kingsley to Günther, plus an envelope on which someone – Mary herself? –

had written 'bird droppings' but which in fact contained a pressed white moth, so tiny it would have been easy to miss it, and, in a sheet of folded notepaper, smeared and streaked brown, some kind of fronded plant material, so maybe *that* was the bird droppings. But why were they in with her letters, rather than with the specimens – the various fish and so on that she brought back from West Africa – that are kept elsewhere in the museum? A little white moth from the French Congo, over 120 years old. Does anyone know it's there?

At the NHM they have a 'clean hands' policy, which means you have to clean your hands with a wet wipe before touching anything. Two more of Kingsley's letters are bound into a fat volume of letters to Günther, and are wrongly catalogued (in the paper catalogue) as being sent from Chiswick. Chiswick? I was puzzled, then saw that the following letter in the bound volume, from some other person completely, comes from Chiswick, so someone has got muddled up. In these two letters Kingsley is asking Günther for preserving spirit – fifteen gallons of it – first to be sent to her flat in Addison Road, but then she changes her mind and asks him to send it direct to the West Africa boat at Liverpool, and please could she have it in *two* containers rather than one, but of course if that's inconvenient…etc., etc. After all the years of self-sacrifice – being a good Victorian daughter looking after her ill mother and typing up her father's notes – she was determined to get exactly what she wanted, disguising that determination behind a facade of feminine flutter and flimflam.

Yesterday I went with Hannah Kanter – my friend since the days of The Women's Press – to the V&A to see the Lockwood Kipling exhibition. On display were original copies of Rudyard's Indian Railway Library series of short story collections, little grey booklets priced one rupee, with cover illustrations by his father Lockwood Kipling. Lovely! Also Lockwood's plaster models for *The Jungle Book*'s illustrations, including a beautiful 'Toomai of the Elephants'. Lockwood championed Indian art and artists, and made the connection between Indian folk art and European medieval art: those organic patterns of beasts, flowers and foliage which themselves had been the inspiration for the Arts and Crafts designs which influenced Lockwood as an artist.

19 February

In the drive to reduce my steroid dose every three weeks, I came down this morning from 12.5 to 10 milligrams of prednisolone.

20 February

My spine and shoulders are burning.

3 March

I spent most of last week rewriting my Travelling Women lecture in the light of comments from Michèle and Jenny at our last Group of Three meeting. My own travelling and writing women are Mary Kingsley, Rose Macaulay and Naomi Mitchison: Mitchison in her (fictional) persona of memoirist Spacewoman, and also as a traveller. All three women perfected the art of rambling (the title of my lecture), both in terms of their going here and there and opening themselves to things happening to them, and also, more importantly, in terms of their writing about their travels. 'Oh, I'm just puddling about,' says Kingsley of her trip to the Calabar River, whereas in fact her eyes are sharp and her ears finely attuned to her surroundings. Mitchison published a travel memoir called *Mucking Around: Five Continents over Fifty Years*. All three women were cunningly artful in their artlessness.

I am now going to put the lecture to one side for a bit and let it rest. I have spent most of this week writing up an article on doing research in the British Library which I shall try out for the 'Freelance' column in the *TLS*.

My agent didn't reply to my last email, so I emailed her again. This time I got a line in response: she's very busy with the London Book Fair and will submit my book once the Fair is over. Originally, she said she would submit it in November, then in January. Now we're in March. Is she ever going to submit it? Whatever happened to the 'deal by Christmas'? Or indeed her notes on the early chapters? I'm beginning to get a really bad feeling about this. How I hate the long silences, and having to steel myself to write an email saying, 'Excuse me, but…', then dreading her response, then my anxiety increasing as the silence lengthens once again. It is exactly what happened with my previous agent over *S is for Samora*. When that agent dropped me I just had to dredge up the confidence to carry on alone. When Michael Dwyer of Hurst said he liked what I had written and was 'minded to publish it', I remember I wept down the telephone.

8 March

International Women's Day. Any celebratory feeling is always unsettled for me by the memory of my first pregnancy ending in miscarriage on this very day. It was years and years ago – well over thirty. A generation ago.

Yesterday I wondered whether it might be worth taking some of the ancient tramadol from my secret stash (expiry date 2010), after a conversation with my mother-in-law, who was prescribed tramadol in place of her normal Oramorph, the latter being, according to her GP, 'potentially addictive' and 'too dangerous'; this for a woman of ninety-six who at times suffers severe pain from nerve damage caused by shingles. This morning I swallowed two from my stash. Have they made a difference to the pain? I think not, but they have given me a dry mouth, deafness, and, yes, that remembered woozy feeling. My mother-in-law took two of hers – which unlike mine are in date – and reported feeling 'unsteady'.

She has offered me hers to try, to see if unexpired ones make any difference to my level of pain. But instead I have increased my steroid dose back up to 12.5 milligrams. Somehow I seem to have dropped out of all medical systems, both local and hospital.

Chapter 5

March – October 2017; Home, Newcastle, London,
Birmingham, Szczyrk, Home

17 March 2017

My essay on the British Library (in which I recall the prize-giving held in the atrium, before the new building had been opened to the public, when Michèle won the WH Smith Literary Award for *Daughters of the House*) includes stuff on portraits, such as the woodcut illustration I found of the 'people of note' interviewed in the Bloemfontein *Friend* when Kipling was editor and when Conan Doyle was doctoring in the field hospital. Kipling and his pals used an old block (an advertisement for hair restorer) that they'd found at the back of a cupboard to illustrate every single 'person of note'. Some of the persons were not amused. (I haven't managed to find out what Doyle himself thought.) I'm also writing about Nick Lord's magnificent portrait of Hilary Mantel, the only living author to have her portrait hanging in the library, and to which I was compared by those identical twins from the Midwest. My idea is to once again try the *TLS* 'Freelance' column. The last attempt I made on that column was with a piece contrasting present-day Croatia with Croatia when it was part of Yugoslavia back in the early '70s when Dad was a British Council rep in Zagreb. Fierce 'Freelance' editor JC returned it to me twice with suggestions for improvement, which I implemented, and then he rejected it outright on the third go. Michèle has helpfully edited a first version of this new one for me, trying to assume a JC-like ruthlessness.

27 March

A glorious, sunny Mothering Sunday yesterday; the clocks went forward and it truly felt like spring. My elegant white tulips are flowering in their pots by the front door. 'I'm sure we didn't order those nasty pale tulips,' said my mother-in-law, whose taste in flowers runs more to the garish. Forsythia, daffodils, primulas and hellebores are all out; fantastic rich yellow pansies in the stone girl's hat. Mum used to fill it with cascades of white when it stood in her backyard. Bumblebees buzz around the bright red flowers of the Japanese quince.

28 March

Nearly four months have passed since I sent a book proposal and three chapters to my so-called agent, as she had requested, so that she could submit them here and there. As I discovered in January, she hadn't sent anything out; indeed, she had not even read the chapters herself. I re-sent them all, and since then I have received a couple of delaying emails, the last one promising that she would send everything out after the London Book Fair. That was three weeks ago.

I need to get back into the book before everything becomes too distant and alien, so I'm going to try to write a draft of the final section (the afterlives or legacies of my three subjects); then go back and start rewriting from chapter 4. I would love some feedback, but must just plough on without it.

29 March

JC has said he'll read my 'Freelance' attempt, so I have sent it off. My heart was thumping as I clicked 'send'. I must try not to think about it.

31 March

RDA AGM. I have been asked if I would like to take on the role of record keeper of the children's achievements. I said, 'Yes please, I'd love to.' I have been so missing my Thursday afternoons at the stables. Missing the smell of ponies and tack and stables, all the pony chat that goes on, the way some of the children laugh out loud when they are trotting.

4 April

No news from JC. Meanwhile, in Graham Swift's *Mothering Sunday* – what a brilliant novel; why didn't it win the Booker last year? I don't think it was even shortlisted – the narrator Jane Fairchild muses, 'What a preposterous word anyway, "trousers".' Could I slip that into my 'Freelance' musings on the phrase 'trousering the cheque', something Michèle was accused of doing by a tabloid journalist the day she won the WH Smith Award and we were all at a luncheon in the atrium of the soon-to-be-opened new British Library? (Michèle was actually wearing a stylish lacy red frock, not trousers at all.) I have already referenced Beachcomber's 'Trousers over Africa'.

Jane's reading of Joseph Conrad at the end of *Mothering Sunday* made me think of sea-loving Mary Kingsley when she allied herself with him, saying, 'There is nothing like us sailormen for literature!'

'Oh, Conrad, I used to love all that seafaring stuff,' says Jane, looking back after a successful writing career to when she was a housemaid 'in service', borrowing one book at a time from her employer's library. Conrad's vision of 'the East' she calls, 'a vision, a promise, a fact, an illusion'. Which contrasts with Dea Birkett's seeming disapproval of Kingsley, and all the other women travellers she writes about, for being English and middle class, and for making up stories: in other words, for having visions and illusions. Birkett seems to feel obliged to berate herself for being attracted to these women: 'increasingly unattractive role models…my admiration for them grew awkward'. Whereas my admiration for Kingsley only grows.

Yesterday was a beautiful spring day, an April day like June; in *Mothering Sunday* it is a March day like June. At Epping Forest Burial Park we placed tulips on Mum's grave in the dappled sunshine. She would have turned 102 yesterday. The ending of *Mothering Sunday* is a tour de force. Perhaps 'we are all secret agents,' thinks Jane. She imagines herself lying in bed next to an ageing Joseph Conrad, the two of them naked, silent, as they watch the smoke from their cigarettes rise and mingle in the still air.

17 April

Easter Monday. I haven't written anything in this journal for two weeks – that is, since the day after returning from visiting Mum's grave in Epping – because for the first week I was writing a draft of the Mary Kingsley chapter of the book's fourth and final section. I can't quite get the ending of it: I would like to end with the anti-colonial campaigning of Alice Stopford Green and Roger Casement, move on to their involvement with E. D. Morel (who wrote some of the best obituaries of Kingsley) and the Congo Reform Association, and from there to Conan Doyle. His *The Crime of the Congo* is powerful, passionate stuff – it must have had quite an effect on public opinion. And wasn't Doyle at the height of his return-of-Sherlock-from-the-dead popularity?

Then during the second week – that is, last week – I was marking the ELCE (English literature and community engagement part-time degree course) Year 2 and 3s' end-of-year essays, which took me the whole week. Well, the whole week with breaks: on Thursday morning, the thirteenth anniversary of Dad's death, C and I took the dog up Dolberrow Hill, from the top of which we had scattered Dad's ashes. I thought of Dad's spirit flying in the wind up there. There was not another person in sight, and although it was a grey day the Bristol Channel shone clear with Flat Island and Holm Island sharp against the water. What has created the wide, smooth green sward that takes you down from the summit? C says it must have been made by people walking on it, but how can that be if there is never anyone here? I believe it has been worn smooth by the nightly passage of the Elf King and Queen and their entourage.

20 April

I have reduced the prednisolone dose to 7.5 milligrams, and what I've got now is an excruciating pain in my left shoulder, neck, and spine, which I'm pretty sure is from repetitive strain injury, exacerbated by hours last week of online marking: clicking and twisting, clicking and twisting, over and over again. It feels different from the PMR pain, besides being unilateral rather than bilateral. It shifts between feeling as if I have a skewer through my shoulder blade to feeling as if my whole upper left torso has been crushed or battered.

24 April

JC has turned down my piece for the *TLS* 'Freelance' column. He wrote, 'Diverting but too diffuse – too many diversions.' Diverting is good, it seems, but not too much of it. I myself believe the piece to be tightly – nay, intricately – constructed. I feel cast down. I write and I write and I hardly ever get published. I haven't heard from my agent for months. She didn't even respond to my sending her the link to the Facebook page that features me as keynote lecturer at the A Suitcase of Her Own conference in Poland. Whereas at the university my boss kindly put up a congratulatory notice about it on the ELCE Blackboard.

I need to finish a draft for the book's final section, then go back to the beginning and start a proper first edit, and then, I suppose, send the book out myself. There's no point in approaching anyone until I've got a whole manuscript to show, one that is as completely finished as I believe possible.

Meanwhile a US educational publisher has asked to reprint my Joanna Russ chapter from *In the Chinks of the World Machine*, and has agreed to pay me a fee, for which I boldly asked, of $500. That has cheered me up a bit.

29 April

I spent most of yesterday answering emails and thereby provoking more of them – but sometimes it just has to be done. An American PhD seeking information on Joanna Russ led to an exchange of three or four emails with Gwyneth Jones, who is just finishing a book on Russ. And I had to mark the final (I think and hope) late submissions from my ELCE students. I have started reading one of the two books on Roger Casement that Michael Wherly has lent me.

2 May

Taking the dog up the lane this morning, I heard, over to my left, from somewhere around Littlewood Pond, a cuckoo. It is the first time a cuckoo has been around here for at least fifteen years.

13 May

Alas! I have not heard the cuckoo again.

21 May

Not another squeak from the agent: vanished like the cuckoo. I suppose I'll have to email her. Again.

23 May

I flew up to Newcastle last week to attend Julia Szołtysek's lecture on Gertrude Bell and orientalism – and (the real reason) to meet Julia in person in advance of the conference in Poland. The lecture was brilliant. Julia is clever, curious, probing, wide-ranging. There were only about ten of us in the audience, but almost everyone had something to say about the feminization of imperialism and suchlike knotty concepts. Later we went out to a Lebanese restaurant with the archaeologist who had organized Julia's lecture and some of his colleagues from archaeology and classics. He was very funny on the subject of going to conferences and noticing the sartorial distinctions between Romanists and Byzantinists: the former in grubby jumpers and jeans, the latter favouring silk scarves and cashmere jackets.

The next morning Julia and I had breakfast together at the hotel and then sallied out and examined in close detail everything on show at the Laing Gallery, which includes a lot of Victorian orientalist painting and also a good collection of Pre-Raphaelites, including Edward Burne-Jones's terrific and sinister *Laus Veneris*. Burne-Jones was Kipling's uncle – married to Alice Kipling's sister Georgiana. Rudyard loved both Aunt Georgie and Uncle Ned. It was his annual visit to their warm and welcoming house in Fulham, when he was a small boy suffering abuse in the 'House of Desolation' where his parents had left him, that kept him going. When he was grown-up he and Burne-Jones were very close.

26 May

I did email the agent, on Wednesday, and have had no response.

30 June

7 milligrams of prednisolone since mid May. I feel so much better for being on a lower dose, despite the painful stiffness in the neck

and hips for the first half of the day. But it's nothing like what it used to feel like: the fiery harness that seared my shoulders; the alien digging its burning claws into my back. This morning I downed a couple of paracetamol and attended a Friday-morning tai chi workshop for the first time in a year.

4 July

To the British Library to look at a run of *The Illustrated London News* from 1900, and then to meet up with Michèle at Waterstones in Gower Street to jointly chair an event with Emily Midorikawa and Emma Claire Sweeney on their book *A Secret Sisterhood: The Hidden Friendships of Jane Austen, Charlotte Brontë, George Eliot and Virginia Woolf*. They are the two young women who invited Michèle and me to write about our friendship for their *Something Rhymed* website, and when we sent them something the length of a short book they just politely and carefully edited it down to the required 800 words. This book explores their own literary friendship, too. Emma wrote a lovely novel called *Owl Song at Dawn*, which was inspired by her autistic sister. I gave copies of it to my friend Rita who runs RDA and to my younger daughter Ismay and they both loved it.

12 July

When I was in the British Library last week I picked up some old copies of the *Friends of the British Library Newsletter*, and when I got home I screwed up my courage and emailed the editor, Lindsay Duguid, who for many years was fiction editor at the *TLS*, and offered her my essay on the BL and portraits, cheque-trousering, identical twins and various other – not necessarily diffuse – matters. Naturally, I didn't tell her that it had been rejected by JC. And she replied, 'Do send it.' So I cut it and cut it, and got it down to 577 words and sent it off. And now…she would like to publish it in the

Newsletter! She said it was 'genuinely interesting and quietly funny'. What an incredibly nice woman! We have arranged to have a coffee together when I'm back in the BL next month.

This has inspired me to write to the British Council to see if they have an internal newsletter or magazine in which I can place my other JC-rejected piece.

20 July

On Monday I drove to the University of Birmingham to visit the Cadbury Research Library to read Mary Kingsley's letters to Colonial Secretary Joseph Chamberlain, excerpts from which are quoted by both Dea Birkett and Katherine Frank. I had no idea where the library was situated, but when I arrived at the campus I saw a group of students sitting on the grass, so I stopped the car and jumped out to ask them. They laughed and said that this was it, the very building behind them, and I just had to go through this gate here to get to the car park. It was blessedly easy.

It was a lovely day, of course, as it always is in a library. The correspondence between Kingsley and Chamberlain was initiated by him when he read an article by her in *The Spectator* in which she criticized British colonial policy in West Africa in general, and the imposition of a Hut Tax in Sierra Leone in particular. She gave him pretty much a crash course in the economic infrastructure of Sierra Leone, and the contemporary failings of colonial policy. In the letters – which are passionate, intimate, engaging – she goes on and on about the absolute central importance for the colonial government of listening to people who have local knowledge and who know what they are talking about, including West Africans themselves. If the government would listen to those over whom it ruled, it could manage them 'without a gun being so frequently brought into the argument'. Chamberlain was a clever fellow, as well as a charmer, and it is obvious from the letters that he was keen to hear what Kingsley had to say, and in particular to hear the evidence that she brought to bear on the subject of the Hut Tax and colonial taxes in general. But he was a politician, and slippery as well as charming (it appears he was more implicated in the disastrous Jameson Raid of 1895 – definitely a provoking incident of the Boer War – than was known at the time), and Kingsley was, not to beat about the bush, only a woman. Even if she did know a lot about West Africa.

But why is there a sixteen-month gap in the correspondence? It wasn't as if Kingsley ever stopped worrying away at all those questions of British colonial policy. Hmm.

In the catalogue I spotted an entry for a handkerchief printed with Kipling's 'The Absent-Minded Beggar' ('When you've shouted "Rule Britannia", / When you've sung "God Save the Queen", / When you've finished killing Kruger with your mouth, / Will you kindly drop a shilling in my little tambourine / For a gentleman in *khaki* ordered South?…'), which he rushed out in October 1899 just after war was declared against the Boer Republics, to raise money for the British troops and their families. I ordered it up: it was a good-sized fine cotton handkerchief, with not just the words of the poem printed on it, but the score for the tune composed by Sullivan (of Gilbert and), a picture of Lord Roberts in one corner, Queen Victoria ('God Bless the Queen') in another, and a map of the two Republics. A pretty fancy hanky! I wonder whether Kipling's 'beggar' was a conventional euphemism for 'bugger', just as 'feck' is now acceptable on British television. Kipling had huge sympathy for the put-upon rank and file of the British Army, and was highly critical of those snobbish officers who despised them. In the end 'The Absent-Minded Beggar' raised over £250,000 for the soldiers and their dependants; Kipling was greeted as a hero when he arrived in Cape Town a few months later.

13 September

Next week I'm flying out to Kraków – if I manage to get my boarding pass out of Ryanair, which is not the easiest of tasks because my ticket was booked for me in Poland – where Julia Szołtysek is going to meet me along with her head of department, Zbigniew Białas, who is the author of a trilogy of novels set in twentieth-century Poland, and also a memoir, called *Nebraska*, of the time he spent as a Fulbright scholar in the American Midwest. They will drive me to Szczyrk (pronounced 'Shtirk' or 'Shteeirk') for the A Suitcase of Her Own conference. My lecture is called 'The Art of Rambling: Journeys Through Space and Time'. It is concerned primarily with Mary Kingsley, Rose Macaulay, Naomi Mitchison and the art of rambling, with a few diversions to take in Octavia Butler, Joanna Russ and Ursula Le Guin. (Definitely too many diversions for JC at the *TLS*.) My thesis is about how some women writers – and also travellers – and in particular Macaulay and Kingsley, use a particular prose style to disguise their own authority and intelligence, and thereby set themselves free to write, and to travel, out beyond the horizons of the male gaze.

I have told Julia she doesn't need to come and meet me in Kraków, as I could catch a train or a bus as the other delegates are doing, but she insists – which is actually very nice and allows me not to worry at all about what to do when the plane touches down. Originally they planned three keynote lecturers: besides me, they have invited Linda Cracknell from Scotland who will be talking about walking, writing and landscape; the third one has had her invitation withdrawn after her increasingly peremptory demands for her husband to be flown to Poland at the conference's expense, and for luxury accommodation for both of them... She is now demanding €700 in compensation for having the invitation withdrawn, and is threatening legal action.

For some weeks now, since before I went to Poland, I've been having severe pain in the neck, shoulders – mainly the rounded bone on my right shoulder – hips, lower back, thighs and knees. It's extremely painful when I wake up in the mornings, and an absolute struggle to pull on pants and socks. But it's not the burning, fiery pain I had originally last year, across my upper back. It's more like a deep ache. I'm having a blood test this afternoon to check that the inflammation markers haven't shot up again; as the pain doesn't feel inflammatory, I suspect they haven't. I have been coughing and sneezing and feeling bone-tired since I got home. I think I picked up a low virus in Poland, or perhaps on the plane, when an old man on the other side of the aisle sneezed so violently that I felt it splattering my arm and the back of my hand. Still and all, I had a wonderful and hilarious time in the ski resort (as it turned out to be) of vowel-free Szczyrk, where the rain poured in waterfalls off the mountains around us, and delegates came from Turkey, Romania, South Africa, and Germany, as well as from Poland. And one from Aberystwyth; I discovered, I think on day two, that she – Rose Simpson, whose conference paper was on the German-Jewish *émigré* writer Vicki Baum – had been, in a previous incarnation, Rose of The Incredible String Band. I'm not sure whether anyone else at the conference apart from Zbigniew (massively knowledgeable about popular culture) had ever heard of The Incredible String Band. As soon as I got home I dug out my CD of *The Hangman's Beautiful Daughter*, and there was Rose on the cover along with the other members of the band, with their long hair and hand-knitted jumpers and assorted small children and dog. Back in the day, I used to own the vinyl LP.

My lecture seemed to go well; Julia and Zbigniew said they would like to include it in the conference collection to be published. It is incredibly confidence-boosting to have someone want to publish what you've written. If it weren't for Julia and Zbigniew, for James McConnachie of *Collected*, for Lindsay Duguid at the BL, every ounce of writerly confidence I once possessed would by now have trickled away.

2 October

The duty doctor rang from the surgery: my CRP is raised, but not by much, from 5 (six months ago) to 10, while my ESR (erythrocyte sedimentation rate in red blood cells – if high, an indicator of high immune protein) remains the same. We agreed that the current pain in my lower back, hips, and knees is probably a consequence of a virus. She suggests that I don't reduce the steroids from 5 to 4 milligrams for another three weeks.

6 October

I have laboured my way back into the book, returning (again) to the first Mary Kingsley chapter, one of the three that I sent to my agent nearly a year ago, and that, in June, as I eventually discovered, she submitted to Bloomsbury. When I reread it I was ashamed of its thinness, its scrappiness.

12 October

I was moaning to Michèle that I feel *stupid* to have embarked on so massive a project as this Boer War book; she generously said no, it wasn't stupid, it was ambitious. I immediately felt better.

On Monday I spent time doing administrative work that had been preying on my mind. First I wrote to Steve Cook at the RLF and withdrew from the consultant fellowship programme. I explained that after a year of dealing with PMR I was still unable to manage the condition with confidence, and that travelling away from home, with the added stress of teaching strange people in strange places, was more than I could cope with. It is not just the crippling morning pain that makes standing in front of rows of beady-eyed graduate students in a seminar room at 9am a nightmarish prospect, but the unpredictable (although invariably exacerbated by nerves) irritated bowels, i.e. diarrhoea. Steve was of course hugely understanding and nice about it. I do feel guilty about having had all that expensive consultancy training lavished on me.

And then I emailed the archivists at the Liverpool School of Tropical Medicine and the Sydney Jones Library at Liverpool University in order to make arrangements to go and read the Mary Kingsley/George Macmillan correspondence and their other Kingsley-related material.

19 October

I bumped into the artist Gail Mason the other day while I was walking the dog up Meeting House Lane. She is very nice, I must say. Things seem to be going well for her: a solo show coming up in March in the Bishop's Palace in Wells, and a number of other joint shows. I told her about the difficulties I was experiencing with my book – the inordinate length of it, the not having a contract with a publisher, the silence of my agent – but how I felt that it was important for me to struggle on. And she said, 'Yes, of course, you want to give it your best shot.' That's an encouraging way of looking at it: I can only do the very best I can, and then *hope* for the best…

I am trying to get the first two Mary Kingsley chapters into narrative order – I mean get the story into shape. I've been thinking about how subjectively or personally one reacts to the stories of other people's lives: how unsympathetic I feel towards – indeed, how lacking in interest I find – the putative romance between Kingsley and Matthew Nathan. I find I am considerably more interested in Mary's close relationships with various women: Violet Roy; Amy Strachey; enigmatic Matilda Goldie, whose early death so grieved Mary; and, of course, Alice Stopford Green, the 'red hot Irish revolutionary' (as she was called by Scotland Yard when they were busy stitching up Roger Casement, as I discovered from one of the Casement biographies that Michael Wherly lent me). Who gives a toss about that stuffed-shirt cold fish Major Nathan? Not Alice. Nor me!

31 October

Halloween. In my rewrite I have reached Mary Kingsley actually disembarking at Cape Town from the SS *Moor* and going to visit Carrie Kipling, alone and lonely in the Mount Nelson Hotel while Rudyard was off having 'Larqs' with his journalist chums in Bloemfontein. The first anniversary of the death of Carrie's beloved first child, Josephine, was just around the corner. Was Kingsley aware of that? I don't know.

John Pilkington, with whom I was an RLF Writing Fellow at Bristol a few years ago, and who like me is struggling with a lengthy writing project, told me he had been cheered by writing an essay for the RLF online magazine *Collected* (that a couple of years ago published my piece on South Africa) and receiving £250 for it. Maybe I'll try and pitch for another one. John's essay was on literary pseudonyms, and it was excellent.

Although we enter November tomorrow, my mother-in-law's bed of glorious orange and gold dahlias and long-stemmed white cosmos is still going strong. The dahlias glow in the afternoon sun, and the cosmos gleam in the early dusk, like little shining moons.

Chapter 6

November 2017 – January 2018; Liverpool, Home

14 November 2017

Liverpool, Hotel 46, Fenwick Street. (You pronounce the 'w'.) Travelling up to Liverpool I met one chatty elderly (probably near enough to me in age!) woman after another. Between Bristol Temple Meads and Birmingham I was sitting next to one who asked a young man across the aisle to turn down the sound on his laptop (which wasn't particularly loud), and then proceeded to shout into her phone, at her husband, 'I don't know where I am. I'll ring you when I get to Birmingham...', and then rattle on loudly to the young woman opposite me (I must have looked too disapproving for her to try to talk to me) about the trials of train travel. When she got off at Birmingham I fell into – quiet – conversation with the woman she had been talking to – good-looking, silvery-coloured hair cut in a bob – who turned out to be an artist working in embroidery and photographs, or rather embroidery or threadwork *on* photographs (I think many of them self-portraits), and who was on her way to give a guest lecture at Manchester School of Art. I discovered later that her name was Jessa Fairbrother.

At Stafford I transferred into a smaller train that was packed with people. I had to sit in one of the seats in the big space outside the lavatory, which fortunately was out of order so we were spared a stream of people going in and out and getting a front-seat view of the actual lavatory every time the door opened. The woman beside me was travelling to Liverpool to attend the funeral of her sister, who was only sixty-three, two years older than the woman herself. A blonde woman, a bit pink in the face and puffed-looking, was sitting on the opposite side of the carriage from us (the locked lavatory in between us): she was returning from staying in London with her thirty-year-old daughter who had just been dumped by her boyfriend of six years because he didn't want to 'settle down'. The daughter had to move out of their nice Oxford flat and was now living in one room in a shared house in Haringey, surrounded by unpacked boxes and very distressed by it all. The three of us were hugely sympathetic to each other's stories, and the journey passed in no time.

Hotel 46 has no other amenities besides actual bedrooms: no lounge, nor bar. The room itself is perfectly OK except for a strange, loud ticking in the corner, inside the wall, as if something in there is expanding or contracting. It doesn't do it the whole time, but it is quite intrusive. The shower stall could do with a bit of maintenance, too.

The Liverpool School of Tropical Medicine (LSTM) holds typescripts of Mary Kingsley's letters to her publisher George Macmillan and his wife – oh, the ease and pleasure of reading typescripts rather than having to figure out the handwriting! The archivist put me in a little side room or office off the main reading room (which was busy with students) and left me alone there with all the files I had ordered. Margaret Macmillan was another of Kingsley's good women friends, I now realize. By the end of 1898 Mary was addressing her as 'Margaret', and reporting on her state of health, her work, and chit-chat about what 'Mrs Green' was up to. She writes to George Macmillan about including the lecture she gave to the Imperial Institute – the last public talk she ever gave – in the next edition of *West African Studies*: 'it is practically a chapter on Imperialism in West Africa'. (It was included as an appendix in the second edition.)

Later I asked if I could see the original Mary Kingsley Medal, which was instituted in Kingsley's memory in 1903 by her friend the Liverpool trader and shipowner John Holt, and is still awarded in recognition of outstanding scientific achievement in the field of tropical medicine. The archivist brought it for me to look at in its glass case. It is a beautiful work of turn-of-the-century art nouveau. The front was designed by Charles J. Allen and shows a bas-relief portrait of Kingsley in profile. The reverse, designed by J. Herbert McNair, who was a brother-in-law of Charles Rennie Mackintosh, and also designed the LSTM's original stained-glass window of a trading ship on the West African route, shows an African man gratefully receiving the benefits of science from a white man.

I wondered whether there would be any record in the LSTM of my grandfather and great-uncle, both of whom, at the turn of the twentieth century, took the diploma in tropical medicine, and both of whom worked on the Gold Coast (as Ghana was then called). The archivist very kindly dug out for me the official LSTM logbook, which was started in 1899. In the back pages it lists all those who took the diploma, including in 1907 George Ernest Hugh Le Fanu (my great-uncle) and in 1908 Cecil Vivian Le Fanu (my grandfather). CV (as he was known) contracted sleeping sickness on the Gold Coast and died of it back home in Bexhill-on-Sea sometime in the 1930s, when my dad was fifteen or sixteen.

On my way out I stopped in the main corridor outside reception to look at the three oak boards that are gilt-engraved with the names of all the recipients of the Mary Kingsley Medal. The most recent is a Kevin Marsh, in 2015. (Later I looked him up: child health in the tropics, especially malaria; worked in Kenya for twenty-five years; now senior adviser to the African Academy of Sciences.)

The university's Sydney Jones Library Special Collections are strictly run: one file doled out at a time, use of pencil or laptop only, under the constant eye of an archivist (although a glass wall divided us readers – just me and one man – from the archivist's desk). Here I saw the originals of the letters I had already read in typescript at the LSTM – so it was a breeze to read them through. There was one long letter that I hadn't seen in the LSTM, written by Mary Kingsley to Margaret Macmillan, from Calabar in February 1895. This was her second trip to West Africa (when she met Roger Casement, although she doesn't mention him to Margaret). She sounds uncharacteristically depressed. 'Friend after friend who I seek after I find is "dead now".' The accompanying typescript had numerous blank spaces, but I was able to identify the missing words so I think I must be getting used to her handwriting.

I found a letter to Kingsley from her agent offering to set up for her 'a good number of really remunerative engagements' if she stayed in England for the autumn of 1897 (which she did). 'I think £200 or £300 could easily be made in that time,' he said, and there would still be plenty of time left for writing.

I also read a bundle of letters, and a large collection of press cuttings, concerning Kingsley's death. It is clear she was hugely liked and admired in Liverpool. Anti-imperialist campaigning journalist E. D. Morel wrote obituaries of 'the truest, kindest, staunchest friend that ever breathed' for a number of journals, including the *British Empire Review*: 'There is something acutely pathetic in the death of Miss Mary Kingsley while engaged in nursing poor delirious wretches struck down by the fatal germs they had imbibed from the pestiferous, carcass-choked waters of the Modder, in the trenches at Paardeberg; nursing them – as one of the last, if not the last, letter she ever wrote, explains – with utterly inadequate assistance, under conditions which rendered the task one of deadly and realisable peril...' Morel, with financial backing from John Holt, would soon set up the Liverpool-based *West African Mail* in which he would reveal the horrors of King Leopold of Belgium's rule in the Congo; he would go on to found the Congo Reform Association, and draw in support from Kingsley's friends Alice Stopford Green and Roger Casement. Arthur Conan Doyle was also involved; Doyle's *The Crime of the Congo* was a stroke of campaigning genius on the part of Morel.

As I went into the Sydney Jones I happened to notice a poster displayed in the anteroom advertising a sale of science fiction books in the room next to the reading room, so, halfway through the morning, getting up to stretch my legs, I went in to have a look around. There I found Andy Sawyer, librarian of the Science Fiction Foundation (which moved to Liverpool from North East London Polytechnic – as was, before it became the University of East London – where I used it while I was writing *In the Chinks of the World Machine* back in the 1980s), whose name I've been familiar with for years but whom I had never before met. He is also director of the MA in SF studies at the University of Liverpool. When I introduced myself, he knew at once who I was, and very sweetly made a sort of gracious salaam in greeting. I was incredibly touched. He told me that the Foundation gets gifted lots of private collections, often by women when their husbands die. They receive mountains of tattered and battered Asimov and Heinlein paperbacks; hence a regular sale.

Where to eat in the evenings, in a strange place when you're on your own, is always a bit tricky. On my first night I asked the hotel receptionist for advice. He said there were lots of chain restaurants to choose from in Liverpool ONE, the big shopping centre down the road, but I really don't like those privately policed shopping centres, especially at night. I had already spotted a shabby-looking pub over the road – The Slaughter House – so I thought I'd try there. There was a big TV screen showing football, only a few other customers, and a nice woman behind the bar drew me a pint of beer and recommended the Scouse stew. I said yes to that, and she sent an older woman – her mother, it transpired – off to prepare it. It was very tasty: meat, potato and carrots in a substantial gravy, quite spicy, with red cabbage. Food and beer came to under £10.

On Wednesday evening I took the train under the Mersey (trying not to think about the thousands or hundreds of thousands – or millions, even – of tons of water overhead) to Wallasey, and went first to New Brighton to have tea with Michael Wherly, who has himself (as Michael Carson) written extensively about E. D. Morel and Roger Casement, including a fine novel about the latter called *The Knight of the Flaming Heart*. Some months ago Michael lent me a Casement biography and an edition of Casement's so-called *Black Diaries*. Both of us then went on to have dinner with Jenny Newman (of my writers' group; what a treat to see her at home in Wallasey) and her partner David Evans. I remember a wonderfully sharp and comic story about the new South Africa that Jenny published in the early days of our writers' group. David, her partner, was imprisoned under apartheid as a member of the African Resistance Movement (ARM), and then left South Africa on a one-way exit permit. When he talks about the Boers it sounds to me like 'Burras'; that's what he and his comrades, sewing mailbags under the hot Pretoria sun, used to call the prison guards, who were all Afrikaners.

On Thursday night, I returned to The Slaughter House. A bowl of delicious lasagne with a small side salad and two slices of garlic toast, and a pint of John Smith's: *£6.40!* It is much more comfortable for a woman on her own to sit in a shadowy, cavernous old pub, minding her own business, than to eat in one of those brightly lit glass-fronted restaurant chains. I felt completely at ease.

24 November

7.5 milligrams of prednisolone, and I felt able to go to the bimonthly tai chi morning workshop in the Kelvin Players Hall for the first time since the summer. We went through the whole Lao Jia form, and then repeated the two final sections more slowly. During our banana break I told one of my fellow students about coming to the hall twenty-seven years ago to watch HB's end-of-term ballet class, during which Ismay, sitting on my knee, picked off one of the plastic flower petals from her cotton hat and, without my noticing, stuffed it up a nostril. Some nostril-streaming months later, in the GP's surgery, when the doctor asked how old Ismay was and I said two and a half, he said, 'Oh, she'll have poked something up her nose, then.' By that time the plastic flower was beyond the reach of a GP with tweezers; Ismay ended up in the General, under anaesthetic.

29 November

A bright, clear, shining day, with frost on the ground this morning. Leaves are still scattered on the oak, but they'll come down in the next wind or heavy rain.

A cheque for $500, for the Cengage reprint of my Joanna Russ chapter from *In the Chinks of the World Machine*. How very pleasing.

13 December

Train home from Paddington: low grey sky, snowy fields. At our Group of Three yesterday Michèle and Jenny encouraged me by saying that they liked the two early chapters on Conan Doyle that I had submitted to them. Secretly, I am tormented by the thought that I am inventing the whole narrative of the book. What really are the connections – political, personal – between Kipling, Kingsley and Conan Doyle? What is my story? But I must just plough on and do my best to get the 'Conan Doyle in South Africa' chapter drafted before Christmas. If I don't carry on now I fear it might all slide into an abyss. Oh God, Christmas is so time-consuming. So much planning and shopping and cooking. So many beds to make and remake, and sheets to wash.

8 January 2018

Yesterday I reduced the steroids from 7 to 6 milligrams, and today I feel very stiff in the shoulders, upper back, upper arms, and legs; walking the dog is effortful. How can 1 milligram make so much difference? I'm going to wait for a few days to see if any other factors are involved (have I got a cold coming on, or some other low virus?) before I go back up to 7 milligrams. I've already regained the puffiness/flabbiness that I lost when I went down to 4. Last week I read an article about some women who lost a lot of weight very quickly. They sort of shrank inside their skins, leaving them with an enveloping surface hanging all over them, which they now have to tuck up and tie away.

19 January

When I was at the hairdresser's with my mother-in-law last week, I told Lindsey that I fancied having my hair cut much shorter than usual, and then we went on to talk about whether I should – at last, after all these years – let it grow out white. Lindsey was enthusiastic about the prospect (she said she thought it would really suit me), and I have to say I think that maybe it's about time. I was thinking back to when I first started getting it coloured: it was in 2002, after I'd been on holiday to Cork and Limerick with Mum and Dad. When I was next in London I showed them the holiday snaps I had taken. Dad took off his specs and held each one up close to his nose. 'This is a nice one of your mum,' he said. It wasn't Mum: it was me. I was wearing a shawl I had borrowed off her, and my hair was not the blonde-gold colour that I had fondly imagined it was, but incontrovertibly white, just like hers. Nearly a decade of hair-colouring passed, and then when Mum died I began to think that perhaps it was time to embrace my white hair now that I had, as it were, moved up a generation. But by then C's mother had moved in to live with us and I just couldn't bear the thought of a totally white-haired household. Now, another five or six years on, I'm thinking, So what? to that. After all, I am nearly sixty-five. And think of the money – and time – I would save.

Mary Kingsley was only thirty-seven when she died. The plaque on her coffin gave her age as thirty-five, but that was because over the years she had managed to fudge the year of her birth so that she appeared to have been born firmly inside her parents' marriage, rather than a mere four days after the wedding. She has often been portrayed as a doughty or eccentric (or both) old spinster, whereas in fact she was a young woman still in the first excitement of flexing her intellectual and imaginative powers, enjoying her first taste of freedom. And golden-haired! (Although admittedly she did hide her hair under an idiosyncratic bonnet.)

Kipling lived until he was seventy when, like Kingsley, he died of a perforated gut (nothing to do with typhoid in his case, but rather the duodenal ulcer that had plagued him for twenty years); Conan Doyle was seventy-one when he suffered a fatal heart attack. Despite the bruising of their reputations in their later years (Kipling's jingoism, Conan Doyle's spiritualism), they died as eminent men, representative of a kind of Englishness (or English masculinity?) that both had worked hard to achieve. Golden-haired Kingsley was a more mercurial figure.

28 January

Ursula Le Guin died at the beginning of last week. She was eighty-eight. I remember my son asking, ten or so years ago, 'What are we going to do when Ursula Le Guin dies?' Meaning, how on earth are we going to cope without new books from her? Now we shall see.

29 January

I somehow managed to get through to the end of the book, some of it in incredibly sketchy form, on Friday afternoon, after weeks of working non-stop at my desk until 6pm every night. On Thursday (or was it Wednesday?) I had a brainwave about how to end the final chapter, chapter 14, which is currently a Kipling chapter: bring it back to his South Africa-inspired work, and say that while in some of it he sacrificed the ambiguities of art to political messaging, he wrote some good stuff too, such as the ever-popular, powerfully incantatory poem 'If—', which was inspired, it is said (by Kipling himself, I think?), by that rascal Dr Leander Starr Jameson, whose failed raid into the Transvaal was a crucial early provocation of the Boers. It might be good to end with that: it would bring it back (neatly, I hope) through Jameson to the imperialist ambitions behind the prosecution of the war, while the ambiguity of the poem – the impossibility of fulfilling all of its 'counsels of perfection' – would exemplify the rich ambiguity of much of Kipling's work; how his ability to unsettle things is overshadowed by the crude Kipling-as-jingo which is the received wisdom about him today.

After I had finished, I realized that I should check that I have the same version of each chapter across all three of the machines I use: the desktop, the laptop, and the USB stick. I had assumed that the versions were all the same. No – oh no, they were not all the same. It was lucky I thought to check. And I had to check that I had incorporated all the most recent sets of annotations, too, and on which version I had done so. What a potential for chaos.

Then I had to amalgamate all the chapters – in their correct versions, naturally – into one file and send it off to my agent. At which point I thought that if she was going to send some of it out (I'm not holding my breath on that front), she would need a new proposal that included an accurate chapter breakdown to go with whatever chapters she decided to send. So I wrote a new chapter breakdown based on the current chapters, and sent it off yesterday teatime.

Now I must go through all my notes on the periods that Kingsley, Kipling and Conan Doyle spent in and around Cape Town, so as to remind myself what it is that I shall be looking out for when I am there next month.

30 January

The approaching research trip to Cape Town is making me feel anxious in a number of ways, at least three of which I am able to identify. I am worried, firstly, about being away from home for ten days with my bowels in their current precarious state, ten days framed – oh, horror – by two twelve-hour flights. Ever since I've been on the steroids and the lansoprazole – eighteen months now – just the very thought of going on a journey seems to provoke a bout of diarrhoea. When I was going to London the other day I parked the car in the station car park and was promptly overwhelmed by the urgent need for a lavatory. I couldn't wait for the arrival of the train in fifteen minutes' time, so I had to rush, stiff-legged and clenched-buttocked, to the garage on the far side of the railway bridge and ask them for the key to use theirs. The lansoprazole is meant to counteract the effect that prednisolone (the corticosteroid) has on the stomach, but whatever it does in the stomach, it certainly does nothing to calm the guts. For years I have suffered from stress-related diarrhoea, but now these drugs have raised it to a whole higher level of unpredictability.

Secondly, I am anxious about physical danger. When Mon and I were in Bloemfontein three years ago we were pretty dismissive of the unwritten but frequently expressed rule by which white South Africans live: go everywhere by car. Since then I have often talked with Mon – who in the intervening period has been back to South Africa four or five times – about how a climate of fear is sustained by the way in which white and middle-class black South Africans sequester themselves and their families away from the majority (poor, black) of the population, thus leaving empty of their presence the public spaces, streets, parks, bus stops and so on, that here we take for granted are used by (almost) everyone. We felt a bit of that fear when – against advice – we took the broken-windowed, slashed-seated, graffitied local train from our Cape Town suburb to the coast at Muizenberg and on down to Simon's Town. I remember the guilty relief I felt at seeing another – one other – party of white passengers (four or five large Germans) waiting on the platform. Nothing bad has happened to Mon during the course of her trips over the last three years, although for some of them at least she has remained within the confines of a conference centre or university (or both), and so she hasn't had the opportunity to wander off through the streets on her own. For some reason, this time I am more anxious about our physical safety than I was three years ago. This came home to me when I leapt at Tanya Barben's offer to drive out to the airport with her husband Heinz to pick us up on our arrival. Usually I enjoy the whole business of queuing up for an airport shuttle bus in an unfamiliar, dusty car park; of being driven through industrial suburbs and wondering where all the people actually live; of stealing glances at the other passengers and wondering what their business is. But this time, no, I wasn't looking forward to it. I was dreading it. And I now realize that I had been angling for that invitation, by sending Tanya a series of emails enquiring about shuttle buses, or whether it would be best to book a taxi in advance, and so on. (Taxis: naturally I am thinking about the businessman from Bristol – my home town! – whose wife was pulled out of a taxi in one of the Cape Town townships – what were they doing there anyway? – and shot dead, *on their honeymoon!*) When Tanya's kind offer arrived, I snapped it up.

So, anxiety about diarrhoea and the availability of lavatories; anxiety about physical safety (attack, kidnap, sudden death...). I suspect these are also manifestations of a much larger, ontological anxiety to do with my book and my research for it. What do I hope to find in Cape Town? Will I find out anything at all? Or will I look in the wrong places and thus miss whatever there is (if anything) to find out?

On my trip to Bloemfontein in May 2015, and then during our stopover in Cape Town on the way back to England, my book existed only in my imagination. I told everyone that I was just going to have a look around; to sniff out, if possible, any scents left by Kipling, by Kingsley, by Conan Doyle, but not to do any actual, in-depth research. Thus I cunningly relieved myself of the burden of expectation: not only other people's, but also my own. Besides that, in 2015, my public-facing role, as it were, was as Mon's companion on one of her work trips, and – through Melanie Walker's generosity – as a tutor in academic writing, which provided me with other work besides doing nebulous research for my nebulous book. In other words, I didn't have to justify myself in terms of research for my own book.

In fact, the trip turned out to be fruitful, inspiring even. I got a sense of the landscape of the Orange Free State, including, near Bloemfontein, the site of the Battle of Sanna's Post, which, when Conan Doyle saw it, was still littered with the pathetic detritus of a battlefield: trampled shoes and hats, abandoned haversacks, the fly-ridden heaps of dead horses. The only sign of the battle when I was there, 115 years later, was the overgrown and neglected cemetery of the imperial fallen, which I found strangely moving. All those dead boys. I also got a clearer sense of some of the events that had previously only been blurry, mainly from the Anglo-Boer War Museum outside Bloemfontein with its extraordinary memorial to the women and children who died in the concentration camps, at the foot of which lie the funerary ashes of the passionate English anti-war campaigner Emily Hobhouse.

Our stay in Cape Town was so brief that our excursions could have been more aptly described as sightseeing than as any kind of research. ('Actually, I'm not a tourist, I'm a travel writer,' says one camel-riding Englishman to another in front of the pyramids, in one of Biff's brilliant early cartoons that Jenny sent me a year or two ago. 'Not another cultural imperialist,' reads the thought bubble coming from the head of their silent Egyptian guide.) Mon and I made a quick dash to Simon's Town, where I led the uncomplaining Mon a merry dance in search of Mary Kingsley's Palace Barracks Hospital, which was there in plain sight but at first unseen by me. We then ambled round the UCT campus with its statue of a seated Cecil Rhodes gazing into the African hinterland, still then in situ, and pressed our noses against the gates to the Woolsack, built by Rhodes for the Kiplings – Rudyard, Carrie and their two younger children (Rudyard's beloved eldest child, Josephine, had died two years previously) – as a winter home and a place for the composition of poetry. Oh yes, and we visited the grand Mount Nelson Hotel, through whose elegant rooms Kipling, Kingsley and Conan Doyle had all passed.

I had begun my preparatory emails before the trip with 'I'm only here just to look around…don't know if anything will come of it…' Protecting myself. Not wanting to take responsibility for my work, to admit agency. This time it is different. This time it is my trip. My research trip, funded by a grant from the Society of Authors, for the book that I am actually in the process of writing. My brain buzzes with doubts like a swarm of flies.

Mon, however, is the ideal travelling companion, as I learned nearly twenty years ago when we took our first trip together, following in the footsteps of Rose Macaulay to Trebizond and the Black Sea. We had some hairy moments on that trip, most particularly when a smooth-tongued carpet-seller in the Grand Bazaar in Istanbul, who spoke English as if he had been at Oxford, turned the key in the lock in the front door of his shop while we were sipping his tea and looking at his carpets. Suddenly there appeared from a side door in a dark corner two heavyset men in suits and dark glasses. I sat blinking like a rabbit, but Mon got us out with some quick thinking and plausible lies about returning to the shop after she had sought permission from her husband to buy the carpet laid out at our feet.

Mon brings her own work with her (this time she is bringing three or four PhD dissertations for a final go-through, and has already timetabled Skype supervisions with the students), yet she is entirely easy about what we do and happy to come with me wherever I want to go. I feel no burden of responsibility towards her, and believe she feels no burden of responsibility towards me. (I mean beyond listening, discussing, chewing things over, and deciding together about things that are appropriate for us to decide together.) We trust each other. And she's strong on things that I'm weedy about, such as driving cars in foreign countries. In that instance I imagine we complement each other, as I like to think ('in what passes for my mind,' as Mary Kingsley used to say) that I am the better navigator, although on reflection I can come up with a number of times when I have got us hopelessly lost: driving round and round a series of roundabouts on the edge of Galway, for example, as we searched for the house of the former priest who was an expert on Rose Macaulay's own ex-priest Gerald O'Donovan; or ending up in the middle of a sinister agribusiness near Nantwich when we were hoping to find the Mozambican economist I had come to interview. Perhaps I am not such a shit-hot navigator after all.

I doubt I could undertake these research trips without Mon's companionship. (Well, of course I *could*, but...) She normalizes them for me. Any whim I follow is a reasonable one in her eyes; if it leads us up a garden path, well, that's just part of the business of research. Amidst all this doubt, in other words, she shows me that it is all right to doubt.

Tanya, with whom we're going to stay, and who has offered to come and pick us up from the airport, is a librarian – now retired and working as a freelance indexer, editor and researcher – who for many years was in charge of the rare books in the UCT Libraries' Special Collections division. These include the Kipling Collection, an extensive if somewhat random (as I would soon discover) hoard of Kiplingiana collected over the years by a schoolmaster called John Scott Ivor McGregor, who donated it to UCT in 1959. The collection includes a lot of visual material: photos, sketches, cartoons, caricatures. I have already seen some of it reproduced in an excellent book on Kipling's time in South Africa by a South African historian (no longer alive) called Renée Durbach.

Tanya herself has written interestingly on Kipling and the time he spent in Cape Town: two or three months every year for eight years from 1900. I was in email touch in 2015, but didn't meet her when Mon and I were whizzing through. When I got in touch with her again in preparation for this trip she was very friendly and helpful. She suggested that Mon and I might like to stay in the flat she rents out: it's part of her own house but with independent access, bedroom, bathroom, kitchen, and a sitting room with extra bed. It was adapted twenty or so years ago for her elderly mother. What a lucky chance for us. I checked with Mon, quickly accepted Tanya's offer, and have now transferred the money in advance.

So, off to Cape Town with a place to stay provided by a Kipling expert; with a promise to be picked up at the airport; with a notebook full of queries, some of which Tanya herself may be able to answer; and, behind me, a book that, while it may not yet have found a publisher, at least exists as a draft. From previous experience

I know that once I have got as far as Heathrow my clutch of worries will begin to sound less clamorous.

Chapter 7

South Africa, February 2018

3 February 2018

In the early hours the plane felt as if it were being buffeted by high winds, lashed from one side to the other, picked up, dropped aside. I came fully awake out of my dozing. You feel it much worse at the back of the plane, one of the cabin crew told me. About twenty minutes before landing at Cape Town – seat-belt lights on, all movement forbidden, cabin crew belted into their own seats behind us – I felt a terrible wrenching in my gut. I didn't dare get up, but clenched my bum tight, tight, tight – I could feel the shit coursing through my bowels. Could I, could I hold it in? Christ – talk about mind over matter. I managed to stay seated until the plane had landed and was taxiing along the runway, then I leapt up with a 'Sorry, I'm gonna be sick' to the seated stewards as I rushed past them. I made it just in time. Oh my God, what if I hadn't?

I emerged shaking and queasy. We disembarked and were made to stand in a corridor for half an hour, after which we were allowed into the immigration hall, where we queued in a snake for a further hour and a half. An hour and a half! Throughout that time we passed only one lavatory, and once you'd passed it you couldn't leave the queue to get back to it or you'd lose your place. By then I had taken two Imodium: nausea-inducing but, more importantly, bowel-stopping. There were eighteen immigration control posts, but only five of them were staffed. The queue numbered in the hundreds.

Tanya and her husband Heinz were waiting patiently for us when we eventually staggered through onto South African soil. Tanya is small, freckled and grey-haired. She looks as if her grandparents might have been Eastern European Jews (as indeed they were). Heinz, by contrast, is pale like Swiss cheese (he is in fact Swiss), very thin and a bit stooped. He must have been a charmer in his youth. He looks quite a bit older than Tanya – ten years at least, I'd say. He may be in his eighties. Both of them have large, generous smiles; they could not have been more welcoming. Heinz was (and always is, as we would discover) the driver; Tanya the navigator. Mon and I sat in the back. Tanya shouts her instructions – we think Heinz is a bit deaf – with a great deal of arm-waving: 'Turn left, turn right,' she shouts, not always correctly. Heinz seems not to mind. They stroke each other's arms. At one point, on Tanya's instructions, Heinz turned down a slip road off the motorway. Tanya readjusted the instructions. Heinz jerked the car to the right, back to the freeway, and stopped on the cross-barred bit of road (the area that you're not meant to stop on or even drive over) as he waited for a gap in the hurtling stream of cars. I was feeling too ill and exhausted to be nervous. I remembered how I had put Mon's life at road-death risk on an earlier occasion: in Mozambique, with the artist Malangatana at the wheel.

Tanya and Heinz live in Vredehoek, a residential area of Cape Town known as the City Bowl, on the slope leading up to the northern face of Table Mountain which rears up vertically (or so it appears) behind the house. In the other direction you can see the Lion's Head mountain, often covered with a thick white mane of fog. Theirs is a single-storey house above a gated yard; you have to climb a short flight of stairs up onto a terracotta-tiled veranda. They share the house with two soppy spaniels and with their elder son, thirty-two-year-old Jacques, and his very young-looking wife Janet. Jacques and Janet run a bee business. Many dismantled hives stand in the yard, waiting to be taken somewhere; plastic containers of honey are waiting to be taken somewhere else; one stack of hives teeters just outside the window of the sitting room of the granny flat where Mon and I are staying; a few bees buzz here and there. Jacques is shouty like his mum and can appear abrupt, but he has a lovely smile like both his parents and is quick to be helpful. (The shoutiness is a family thing, I reckon, like Mon's Iranian family who all shout much more than a quiet Englishwoman like me is used to. The other day I heard an Italian comedian on Radio 4: 'The English have so many words for making a noise: "shouting", "crying", "yelling". In Italy we call it "having a conversation".')

We have been warned about the water shortages. After three years of drought, very little water is left in the reservoirs. You must shower only once a day, and only for two minutes, and you have to keep that water to flush the loo when you've done a poo. You're not meant to flush it for a mere pee. Clothes-washing is a problem: I am grateful to Ismay for insisting I bring enough knickers to last the whole trip.

When we arrived we found Tanya had organized lunch to be ready for us on the big wooden table on the veranda: salads, cold chicken, cheeses and breads. Tanya and Heinz always sit close together at one end of the table, so they can lean against each other, hold hands, steal kisses. Mon and I were sitting opposite Jacques and Janet. I dropped my napkin (by accident), and when I bent down to pick it up I saw their bare feet entwined beneath the table. We are surrounded by lovebirds.

I knew nothing about Tanya's background, but I gathered bits and pieces of it over the next ten days. Her mother, Ray Alexander, was a communist, a trade unionist, and for some years the general secretary of the Food and Canning Workers' Union. She married

123

Jack Simons, a fellow communist and lecturer in African studies at UCT. I remember years ago coming across one of the books they wrote together, *Class and Colour in South Africa, 1850–1950*, but I can't remember if I actually read it. Both of them were active in the anti-apartheid underground, until they were forced into a long exile in the 1960s, first in England and then in Zambia, where their house in Lusaka became a meeting place not only for the ANC in exile, but also for cadres from other Southern African countries fighting for independence. Ray and Jack stayed away from South Africa for twenty-five years, returning in 1990 when the ANC was unbanned and Nelson Mandela released from prison.

Tanya was sixteen when her parents went into exile. She was left behind in Cape Town with her elder sister, but her brother, who was only two years younger than her, went off with their parents at the end of 1965, in order to avoid future conscription into the South African Army. In a paper she wrote for a Kipling conference back in the 1990s in which she explored Rudyard's experience of being abandoned by his parents, Tanya made reference, movingly, to her own feelings of having been abandoned.

5 February

This morning Tanya offered to accompany us to the UCT Special Collections. Jacques drove the three of us to the downtown campus from where we would take the university bus to the upper campus. The blue university shuttle buses have 'JAMMIE SHUTTLE' in big letters on their sides: they are named for 'Jammie' Hall, the central building on the upper campus, which is short for Jameson Hall. While the statue of Cecil Rhodes on the upper campus has been pulled down and the 'Rhodes Must Fall' campaign continues, the students and teachers still ride around for free in a shuttle bus called 'the Jammie', whose name commemorates Rhodes's bestest

124

friend, keen imperialist, and co-conspirator in the infamous Jameson Raid of 1895, Dr Leander Starr Jameson.

Tanya took us into Special Collections, introduced me to the librarians, and then took Mon and me down into the stacks to give us an overall view of the Kipling Collection. She showed us a filing cabinet stocked with folders, each one of which contained just one photocopy, letter or cutting. Then she started looking for the 'tickler box'. What on earth is a tickler box? I was wondering. It's an old-fashioned box for index cards with a hinged lid that snaps down over the front. I've got one at home somewhere, probably with some ancient index cards still inside. I never knew that that was what it was called. Various other boxes were scattered around, but not the one for the Kipling filing cabinet.

Back upstairs in the reading room, Mon settled down with her laptop and I started looking at the items I had ordered online in advance, mainly scrapbooks of press cuttings, created by Mr McGregor, the collector.

About an hour later Tanya reappeared triumphantly bearing the missing tickler box. It contains two sets of almost but not quite identical index cards, written out in McGregor's careful hand, some with later additions in another hand. But my heart sank. The entries looked so...arbitrary, I suppose: one particular poem in endless different copies, lots of copies of musical scores to different poems, random reviews of this or that. None of this material is detailed in the online catalogue.

6 February

I felt stronger this morning, and pretty much recovered from the anti-diarrhoea pills I took on Sunday, which always produce a two-day queasiness. OMG, it is hot – what joy to be spending the day in a library. Mon and I took the bus up to the UCT campus and I made a proper attempt on the Kipling tickler box, and started ordering up the folders that it indexes. Yesterday Tanya dug out for me a 1962 pamphlet by the then-librarian, a Mr Immelman, that describes and annotates the collection, and which was withdrawn from circulation after objections by Elsie Bambridge, the only one of Kipling's three children to survive into adulthood, and the guardian of his estate. (I suppose John was officially an adult, but only barely: he had just turned eighteen when he was killed at Loos in 1915.) In the pamphlet I found a photo of the Kiplings taken on board the SS *Kenilworth*, sailing from Cape Town in 1907; it is very similar to one that is widely reproduced in books about Kipling. In the latter, John, aged nine, sits cross-legged on the deck next to his elder sister Elsie, in front of a group of adults. In the photo reproduced by Immelman, John is standing immediately in front of his father, packed in tight among the adults. It looks as if Rudyard has his arms around his son, although you can't quite see because of the crowd. I managed to track it down in the index cards (under 'P' for 'photo'), ordered up the folder, and opened it to find only one print: one of the *other* photograph, the one that everyone knows, with Elsie and John sitting on the deck together in front of the grown-ups. Annoying! I pointed out the discrepancy between the two photographs to the librarian on duty, a sun-wrinkled woman with long white hair, but I'm not sure that she could actually see the difference, or for that matter give a damn. A number of the folders have their indexed contents missing.

The librarian later offered to take us downstairs – not to the stacks, but down the main stairs to visit the Kipling Room, which in fact Mon and I had already seen, the last time we were here in 2015. I accepted the offer politely, although I know the room is dull and actually has nothing whatever to do with Kipling beyond housing some old sets of some of his works in glass-fronted bookcases around the walls. 'Kipling Room' is inscribed in big gilt letters over the doorway, but it is not as if he ever sat here to write: the room didn't exist until the university moved to its present site on the slopes of Table Mountain in 1928, twenty years after Kipling's final visit to South Africa. The librarian was going on about how the collector, McGregor, must have been completely mad, and what a way to spend your life...which sounded a bit odd coming from a librarian, and indeed from one of the custodians of the very collection McGregor had created.

I asked whether I could photograph the room, to which she said she would have to ask permission, because it was all very sensitive these days because of who Kipling was, and if the students found out... Found out what? That there's a 'Kipling Room'? A Kipling Collection? What would they do? Presumably the room was set aside for the collection, which is now quite rightly housed in the archives. If the university authorities wish to avoid trouble, maybe someone should remove the gilt lettering from over the doorway.

Although, since we were last here, the egregious Rhodes statue in front of the university buildings has been toppled and removed, there remains close by the 'Rhodes Memorial', which consists of a massive bust set in a neoclassical temple high above the UCT campus, on a ridge that runs down between the north and south flanks of the mountain. All this land once belonged to Rhodes. Tanya had suggested that we meet at 4pm for a cup of tea in a café which apparently is popular with walkers, tucked away behind the memorial. Mon and I set off in good time across the campus – past some red-brick buildings and some layered with cement stucco, all covered in Virginia creeper (I think the design was based on the University of Virginia, founded by Thomas Jefferson); past groups of students, white, black and brown, all mingling together, unlike at UFS (although the way the students hung out together there, in racially distinct groups, may well have been a consequence of the teaching being done in parallel language streams: there is no Afrikaans stream at UCT); past the now-empty plinth where

Rhodes sat during our first visit three years ago. We were heading towards where I assumed we would find the path that went up the mountain to the memorial. But it wasn't signposted. Or maybe the students had removed the signs? At the far end of the campus, on the edge of a car park, we saw an information kiosk. The two middle-aged women behind the desk threw up their hands in horror when we asked for directions to the path to the Rhodes Memorial: no, no, two ladies like us could not possibly walk along the path; it was much too dangerous. Women were often mugged, or stabbed, or…they didn't actually *say*, 'raped'. It was all right if you were in a large party, you'd be safe then, but the two of us – no, on no account. We *must* go by taxi. They gave us a card for a taxi.

We walked up the slope to the top of the car park, where we guessed the path must start, and Mon did try to call the taxi number – we both felt a bit rattled by the two women's insistence. The number didn't work, so I asked a big white man sitting behind the wheel of his big white SUV (he had the engine running, as if for a quick getaway) whether we were using the right code to make the phone call, and explained that we were looking for the path to the memorial. He climbed out of his car and asked a campus security guard who had just appeared from around the corner if he knew where the path started. Yes, he did, and it was only a few metres from where we were standing. It would have been utterly ridiculous not to take it.

Very steep hillside, blazing sun, no cover, drenched in sweat, dragging one foot after the other: if an evildoer had rushed at me I couldn't possibly have run for my life (when out on lonely walks at home, I sometimes indulge in a worry about wolves being reintroduced to the British countryside, and how I would just have to sit there and wait to be eaten up). But it was only about 200 yards up to a clump of trees – and there, hidden by the trees, was the memorial. Within shouting distance of the campus, really. If we had taken a taxi we would have been driven a mile or two, or more, to get somewhere that was only five (or in my case ten or fifteen) minutes' walk away.

Tea room, but no Tanya. I called her but caught only a word or two about traffic and running late, so I said, 'Don't worry, please don't come if it's difficult – we'll get the Jammie back down to town.' No, no; they were on their way. Mon and I had tea and scones at a shady wooden table among a smattering of other tea-takers, all of whom were white, whereas the staff were all black, as is so often the case in South Africa. Then we walked round to the front of the monument, which was erected soon after Rhodes's death in 1902 and carries an epitaph by Kipling. Rhodes's nose has been chipped off, and 'blood' (red paint) runs down from his left eye. Kipling's lines come from the verses he wrote that were recited over Rhodes's burial place in the Matopos Hills in Zimbabwe (not recited by Kipling himself: he was too distraught to attend the funeral): 'The immense and brooding Spirit still / Shall quicken and control. / Living he was the land, and dead, / His soul shall be her soul!' Hmm. Not one of Kipling's sharper poems. On the paved square below the monument stands an equestrian statue designed by G. F. Watts as an allegory of something or other. Mon and I stood at the top of the steps, looking out as Rhodes did, and admired the panoramic view: Table Bay to the north, False Bay to the south, Cape Flats stretching out to the east in front of us. Rough grass pushed up between the paving stones below and around the prancing allegorical statue. The whole site was gloomy and dilapidated. There was nobody else around. We heard the café close, and cars start up as the staff headed off home. Five o'clock, 5.20, 5.30. We were in the middle of a dark wood with not another soul in sight. I was beginning to feel a bit spooked. Eventually we heard a car stuttering up the mountainside. It came into sight and wove its way to a halt beside us. Heinz sat, smiling, behind the wheel. Tanya, he said, was coming up through the woods with the spaniels.

7 February

We set off on foot for the National Library of South Africa (NLSA), via a local car-hire place recommended by Jacques, where we were told there were no cars available, which was just as well as all their cars are VW Beetles with the phrase 'Fun Car' in amusing font all over them, which we felt would have been somehow inappropriate.

The NLSA stands at the bottom of the Company's Garden (the Company being the Dutch East India Company), and is modelled on Cambridge's Fitzwilliam Museum. Inside it was lovely and cool. The archives room has beautiful wooden bookcases, and tall floor-to-ceiling windows in bays along one side that look over the lush greenery of the gardens. Very quiet, of course, with just the whirring of electric fans, and only a handful of readers.

The archivist had dug out a whole load of Mary Kingsley material for me – things that I hadn't known were there – as well as having ready for me the Hatty Johnson correspondence which I had ordered in advance. The Johnson letters were bought for £350 from an antiquarian bookseller in London in the 1980s. There is no South Africa connection: all the letters date from long before Kingsley's arrival in South Africa. Hatty was the sister of a Cambridge friend of Mary's brother Charley, and seems to have never left Cambridge. Mary wrote to her from the Canaries in 1892 and from Old Calabar in 1895 (during her second West Africa trip) – vivid, exuberant letters. They came with typescript copies, for which, as always, I was grateful.

We had lunch in the café/restaurant in the Company's Garden – pleasant, busy, and a tiny bit racially mixed (the customers still predominantly white, the staff still predominantly black). The gardens are overrun with the grey squirrels that were introduced by Rhodes – what an idiot – and full of exotic trees brought back from the Company's extensive empire. We came home via another car-hire place, where we arranged to pick up a car on Saturday in order to drive to Simon's Town.

8 February

We returned to the NLSA and I read through *Black & White* – an illustrated weekly – for the first months of 1900. The periodical is so named for its photos and illustrations, all in black and white, and provides a fantastic pictorial history: sieges, battles, hospitals, photo portraits of the dead and wounded. I had been happily taking photos on my phone, and then suddenly thought that it would be polite to ask the archivist's permission. I assumed she would say yes, because these pictures are over 100 years old: there are no copyright issues. But she said no, it was forbidden: a blanket rule. And I wonder if it's because of this sensitivity about how recent (or recentish) history (which definitely includes the Boer War) shapes the present. People are worried about how historical stuff might be used. Everyone is tiptoeing on eggshells.

An hour or so later, I found a small photograph of Solomon Plaatje in Mafeking, in a group with two white men in Army uniform and two African runners. Plaatje was the first black African in the whole volume to be named in a picture caption; it gave just his surname, spelled 'Plaachi'. I looked around, saw that the archivist was not at her desk, and I just could not resist. Mon, facing the door, kept cave for me, and I sneaked a photo with a shaking hand. Doubtless I have been caught on CCTV. And then I found a cover illustration of some kind of makeshift tribunal or outdoors court during the Mafeking siege, with the same two moustachioed white men in charge seated behind a desk, and Plaatje leaning against a wall behind them, wearing a beret at a rakish tilt.

Further on in *Black & White* I found a sketch, captioned 'Green Point, site of the POW camp', showing, behind barbed wire, rows of bell tents marching in an orderly fashion back towards Signal Hill, with a flank of Table Mountain on the left. For months I had thought that the POW camp that Arthur Conan Doyle records having visited was the one at Simon's Town, the typhoid-stricken inmates of which were transferred to the Palace Barracks Hospital where Mary Kingsley was working. I had thought that Green Point was the name of the Simon's Town site, but it was only when we got here and I saw it on the Cape Town maps that I began to think, Of course, there must have been other camps – probably one in Cape Town, and, as Doyle was in Cape Town for only a single day before he re-embarked to sail on to Port Elizabeth, that's the one he would have visited. Charles Blasson, too (one of the medical students helping Doyle and the other doctors of Langman's Field Hospital), records taking a tram from the docks to a POW camp which was only twenty minutes away. It must have been the same one, and here was a drawing of it. Instead of photographing the sketch I made a rough copy in my notebook of the outlines of the hills behind the camp, to help identify it if no traces remain on the ground.

9 February

This morning, from my bedroom window, Table Mountain was invisible behind thick grey cloud, which slowly lifted. When the cloud is white and hangs from the summit in vertical folds, they say the Table has on its tablecloth. This afternoon, as we came back across the sea from Robben Island, a slab of dark cloud was obscuring Table Mountain's top; it looked heavy with rain. But is it? Or is it just teasing?

Mon had very cleverly, via her phone, booked us on the trip to Robben Island. No two ways about it: I couldn't manage without

Mon. The boat ride made me queasy. The information film broke down after only a few minutes, adding to both my queasiness and my anxiety. Tanya and Heinz told us later that there had been a recent capsizing of the Robben Island boat; I am glad I didn't know that beforehand.

We were driven round the island in a beat-up old coach, with a tour guide whose English was not easy to follow. Sitting behind us was an extremely noisy boy of six or seven, whose Scandinavian parents, poor things, tried their utmost to keep him quiet. Robben Island is a desolate, scrubby, sandy, shelly, barren place; nothing grows save for low, windswept eucalyptus. We passed the broken grave markers of the lepers, from when the island was a leper colony. We passed the shadeless quarry where the prisoners under apartheid – Nelson Mandela among them – dug and broke stones. At the prison buildings we were handed over to another guide who was extremely articulate and more audible. He claimed that he himself had been an inmate, a political prisoner. He didn't look more than about fifty so he must have been very young when he was incarcerated. Both guides talked about how Mandela and his comrades chose the path of forgiveness and reconciliation, and how important that was for South Africa. It must have been difficult to see your erstwhile captors and guards – men who had beaten you and taunted you and called you 'kaffir boy' for twenty years – walking around the streets of Cape Town. We took our leave of the guide at the gates of the prison compound. He said, 'You are free to go home now.' Yes, indeed. How fortunate we are. What a ghastly place. It reeks of centuries of banishment and punishment. And across the water, visible but unattainable, the strange beauty of Table Mountain and the glinting lights of Cape Town.

We Ubered home from the waterfront. Since Mon cleverly downloaded the app and worked out how to use it, it has been fantastically easy. Everyone – of course I mean every white person –

Ubers here. Most of the Uber drivers, it seems, are from Zimbabwe (two out of our three so far).

10 February

Mon was mugged today as we were walking to the National Gallery. Her two thin gold necklaces, one of which had been her mother's, were wrenched from around her neck.

We had had a very successful morning: we picked up the hire car that we booked on Wednesday, and Mon bravely drove us (thank God I didn't have to!), under my navigation, round to Green Point. We had to move from one busy, screeching highway to another, and so that we could draw breath and get our bearings, I suggested we pull into the lane that pointed to 'Parking for McDonald's Only'. We parked. To our right loomed a huge stadium that was built in 2010 for the World Cup, behind us stood the universal 'M' for McDonald's, and there in front of us, astonishingly, I saw the exact configuration of Signal Hill with Table Mountain that I had seen in *Black & White* and copied into my notebook. I could hardly believe my eyes. We got out of the car and found a tourist information board erected on the grass beside the park. It told us that, back in the day, the building now housing McDonald's had been the grandstand for the nineteenth-century racecourse, that the racecourse was exactly where we were standing, and that it had been converted into a bicycle track when the races moved elsewhere sometime in the 1890s. No mention that this was once the site of a British military camp for Boer POWs. I suspect that the nationalist governments during the apartheid era had no wish to commemorate such things, and since then the ANC have had more pressing things to deal with.

Conan Doyle says in his memoir that the camp was situated on an old bicycle track. By sheer chance we had arrived at the actual site. Doyle was considerably more sympathetic to the Boer enemy than was Kipling. He described the prisoners here at Green Point, to whom he distributed cigarettes and chocolate, as 'a shaggy, dirty, unkempt crowd but with the bearing of free men'.

We returned to Vredehoek, left the car outside Tanya's house, and set off on foot for the National Gallery, avoiding the traffic-clogged main road by cutting though some backstreets. Why, oh why did we not drive? We were walking through a typical middle-class area: substantial houses behind whitewashed walls overhung with frangipani; armed response warning signs; a newly built, gated apartment block. A dog-leg of short streets; bright sunshine. I was ambling along the left-hand pavement, a few feet ahead of Mon. (I can feel the anxiety rise as I type this.) Four men came around the corner ahead of us, walking in a group in the middle of the road, casually but not poorly dressed, aged maybe late twenties or early thirties. Quite bourgeois-looking, but four men nonetheless, and so, as I and countless other women would do anywhere in the world, I dropped my gaze so as to avoid eye contact. We passed each other. One second later, behind me, Mon screamed. I turned and saw one of the men leaping away from her, holding something glittering in his upraised hand. The other three stood around her in a loose semicircle, and in the next second they all ran off round the corner.

I raced back to Mon. I thought that they had grabbed her rucksack – with her handbag inside it – but they hadn't. The man I had seen with something glittering in his hand had torn her two thin gold necklaces from around her neck, leaving her with a bloody scratch. Within moments a young, uniformed man from the gated apartments on the other side of the road ran out. We gabbled an explanation of what had happened, and he immediately set off running after the men. Two youngish white couples emerged – concerned faces, muttering about the police – and then they got into a car and drove away. When I turned around I saw that another (older) white woman had come out onto the veranda of her house, on the same side of the road as we had been on; she gave me a dirty look and went back in again. The young security guard returned from his hopeless pursuit – I was pleased to see him because I was worried he might have been attacked – and rang his boss at the security firm.

Mon was amazingly calm. We kept asking the guard if we should call the police, but it was all a bit confusing. Another woman came out of the gated compound and was sympathetic, but nobody wanted to have anything to do with it, except for the security guard who had so bravely chased the muggers. Later I thought that all the white people probably thought we had got what we deserved for brazenly walking along a street. The security boss turned up in his car. He sucked his teeth when we asked if he thought we should go to the police, and told us that the nearest police station was a long way away… In the end, we accepted that it would be pointless. The necklaces would never be recovered. But the point would be to have it logged that this had happened. These things are not logged, because everyone says, 'What's the point of going to the police?' And so no record is kept, no analysis made. The security chief gave us a lift in his car to the National Gallery. He told us to never, *ever* again walk along empty residential streets.

Mon and I agreed that we would not tell Tanya and Heinz about the mugging. It feels too…complicated. And we wouldn't want them to feel upset on our behalf.

Tonight we took them out to supper as a small thank-you for their hospitality. The four of us walked down to the Portuguese bar/restaurant on the corner, avoiding the seventy-four-year-old white beggar who lives on the street (Tanya: 'and urinates and defecates on it'). He refuses to go to the homeless shelter because it is full, as he puts it, of 'bloody kaffirs'. We had amazing, huge lumps of delicious steak, delicious vegetables, two delicious puddings to share, and a bottle of wine, for R803 – less than £50. And we took home Heinz's leftovers in a doggy bag. Tanya and Heinz sat next to each other, cooing, kissing and stroking in full lovebird mode; without knowing they were doing so, they calmed us down and cheered us up.

11 February

We left Vredehoek at 9.30 this morning. It turned out that the direct route to Glencairn – a few miles up the coast from Simon's Town – meant driving up and over some ruddy mountain that I hadn't even noticed on the map when planning the route. It must be the southern flank of Table Mountain. The hire car, a Hyundai, is even more decrepit than our Nissan at home and has considerably less engine power; it struggled and panted up the steep bends of the mountain road, with Mon heroic behind the wheel.

The seaside hamlet of Glencairn, at the foot of Elsie's Peak, is (I am certain) the Glengariff of Kipling's story 'Mrs. Bathurst'. We parked next to the beach, and I took out my swimming costume from the back seat. Here, in a guards' brake van on a railway siding, with the sea in front of them, Kipling has Pyecroft and Pritchard recount the story of 'Click' Vickery and the object of his obsession: the enigmatic, eponymous Mrs B. During the Boer War, according to a booklet I picked up later in the Simon's Town Museum, a spur line was constructed on Glencairn beach from which the Royal Navy test-fired rail-mounted naval guns.[5] The railway siding is probably long gone – we couldn't find it – but the main line from Cape Town to Simon's Town, which Mon and I took (against all advice) in 2015, has been so buried by the wind-driven sand that it is no longer in operation. The main line has basically become a sort of sand-drifted siding itself. The track now stops at Fish Hoek,

5   *Glencairn Gleanings*, edited by John Clifford, 2003, Simon's Town Historical Society.

the little beach station to the north of Glencairn. Will it ever be reinstated? Yet again, poor (i.e. black) people are effectively denied access to parts of their own country.

A large noticeboard stood by the path that led through the drifting dunes. 'Shark observation,' it said in big letters, and tabulated recent shark sightings off Glencairn beach. I thought that the information was for the benefit of interested shark-spotters; maybe there were clubs and organizations up and down the False Bay strand keen on shark-spotting just as everyone is so keen on whale-spotting in the Pacific Northwest. No, thought Mon: more likely a dire warning. I decided against a swim.

The Central Hotel Guest House on Main Street in Simon's Town is a few yards along from the British Hotel, where Mary Kingsley stayed when she arrived in Simon's Town at the beginning of April 1900. The British Hotel still has a blue-and-white awning over the entrance, stretching across the width of the pavement, with the hotel's name printed on it, but iron gates bar the entrance and the reason that my phone calls – seven or eight of them – weren't answered is that the hotel is closed, sold up. I would have loved to stay there, but the Central Hotel Guest House is of the same period – 1898 – and retains many of its original late-Victorian features. Our bedroom has a high, wood-panelled, white-painted ceiling with a large, rackety fan that keeps the air circulating and makes me think of Raffles Hotel in Singapore (as seen in old war films on TV); and a high, moulded dado rail at the level of the top of the tall window that opens out onto (or would if it could, but as this is South Africa all windows are permanently locked shut) an inner first-floor courtyard with old-fashioned ironwork tables and chairs, and pillars entwined with scarlet bougainvillea. A wide corridor, almost a hallway, with a polished wooden floor leads from the inner courtyard past our room to the balcony at the front of the building, which overlooks the naval yard, and the bay. Where the British Hotel balcony sports elegant fin-de-siècle metalwork, the Central Hotel Guest House, with its plain wooden-fenced balcony, has perhaps more of a Wild West air to it. On the other side of the road are naval buildings, behind a high brick wall to which is affixed a small plaque to Rudyard Kipling, commemorating his various visits to Simon's Town and his lifelong interest in the Navy. He first came here when he was twenty-five, long before the outbreak of war: he was fleeing depression and a nervous breakdown, and on the voyage out he met up with a naval captain called Edward Bayly, who was on his way to Simon's Town and invited Kipling to visit him there. They had a high old time together and Bayly became a close friend.

'No problem with leaving your car parked outside on the road,' said sweet-voiced Shami at the reception desk this afternoon; 'it'll be perfectly safe with the Navy here.' Indeed, there are a number of smart-uniformed men and women walking busily to and from the naval yard.

In Kipling and Kingsley's time, Simon's Town provided a base for Britain's Royal Navy; now it is the base for the South African Navy. False Bay, and Simon's Bay within it, unlike Table Bay, are protected from the stormy South Atlantic by the Cape Peninsula. The whole street frontage – the Central Hotel Guest House, the British Hotel, all the shops in between – looks exactly the same as in the press photographs of Mary Kingsley's funeral cortège on 4 June 1900.

This evening Mon and I sat in wicker armchairs on the hotel balcony with a bottle of local white wine as the sun set dramatically behind the mountains to the north and west of the bay and, as we do so often and so pleasurably, we talked long and loud of this and that.

12 February

Cyril Ramaphosa, since December president of the ANC, gave a public talk in Cape Town yesterday. He has rejected Jacob Zuma's 'conditions' for resignation; it looks as if Zuma might be ousted from the presidency of South Africa within the next few days.

We visited the Simon's Town Museum again. In the biographies of Mary Kingsley there is some confusion or discrepancy about whether after her death her body was moved from the hospital to the military barracks, and about where the funeral cortège started out from. I had brought with me a copy of a press cutting (that I found in the Sydney Jones archive in Liverpool) that showed a rear view of the cortège coming down a steep road, past a house with four chimneys. I couldn't see how this tallied with any of the roads leading from the hospital – perhaps it led from the barracks? I showed the cutting to the volunteer museum guide, and asked if he could identify the road or the house. He thought he recognized the chimneys on the house, and that it might be up at the top of Arsenal Road.

Up Arsenal Road we whizzed, parked the car, and I got out, clutching the press cutting. Yes! We were looking down on the back of the very same house with four chimneys: not far from the Palace Barracks Hospital, but higher up the hill and a little bit further into town, which confirms that the cortège did not leave from the hospital, but from somewhere higher up, which is where the Army barracks must have been. We were standing pretty much exactly where the photographer must have been standing on that Whit Monday in 1900. In my mind's eye the scene unfolded: the cortège, including a detachment of gunners in bright blue tunics and white helmets, and a military band playing the 'Dead March', winding slowly down the steep slope; Kingsley's coffin draped in a Union Jack, the men leaning back against the weight of the gun carriage on which it was placed, to stop it escaping and rushing past them down the hill.

I felt inordinately pleased.

13 February

After breakfast in a pretty little room off the wooden balcony – we could have had it on the balcony but basically there is more blazing sun than I can cope with – Mon and I strolled down to the harbour and to the end of the concrete jetty, from where you can look across to the erstwhile Palace Barracks Hospital, now the admiral's house, which Commander Steyn had shown us round in 2015. In 1900 the jetty was made of wood. It was from here that Mary Kingsley's coffin was lifted from the gun carriage onto a torpedo boat which set off towards the deep water beyond Cape Point. When the boat stopped and the coffin was lowered into the water, it refused to sink and floated off gaily on the waves; the captain and some of his crew leapt into a lifeboat in hot pursuit, and snared the coffin, pirate-style, with a grappling hook. They then tied the line to an anchor and threw it overboard, and so Kingsley's coffin was dragged down beneath the waves.

We drove through the town to its southern or western end, to the site of the Bellevue POW camp, now a golf course. Skirting the golf course, we walked down a scrubby path to Windmill Beach, emerging beneath the outflung branches of an ancient-looking tree onto a sandy cove with two small bays either side of a heap of huge grey boulders. It was exactly as shown in the photos we had seen in the museum, lacking only bearded Boer captives paddling in the shallows behind barbed wire. In the opening scene of Kipling's story 'The Captive', the British militiamen sit in their cutter at the mouth of the bay, 'spanking' the sparkling water with their paddles. Kipling doesn't tell the reader why they are doing that, but I discovered the reason yesterday, in the museum: it was to frighten off any approaching sharks. They also had shark nets draped between the boulders on either side. Even so, Mary Kingsley recorded one poor prisoner killed by a shark; there may have been others. Kingsley was full of respect for the patients in her care: the big, gruff, bearded family men, and their skinny, frightened teenage sons. Unlike Conan Doyle and Kipling, she could understand their passionate attachment to the land, and their view of the British as a greedy invading force trying to steal it.

Before our return to Cape Town we decided to take a look at Cecil Rhodes's seaside cottage just outside Muizenberg. Kipling visited Rhodes in this cottage almost every day as Rhodes lay dying of dropsy in the early months of 1902. After he died his body was taken by train, at night, back to his house, Groote Schuur, in Cape Town on the slopes of Table Mountain. The seaside cottage is now the Rhodes Cottage Museum. By a little gate at the side of the garden wall, people were queuing up with large plastic jerrycans to gather water – which a sign said was non-potable – from the 'Rhodes Stream' that runs down past the cottage. Inside, we joined two other pairs of tourists. The narrative of the displays throughout the museum is pretty upbeat, as one might imagine it would be. Our volunteer guide was a white Zimbabwean who had been a magistrate back in the days of Rhodesia. He had left for South Africa in 1983, three years after Zimbabwean independence, almost a decade before the dismantling of apartheid in South Africa. He held Rhodes in high regard. Well, he would, wouldn't he?

I wanted a final view of False Bay; I wanted to look out southwards for the last time, to the place where the Atlantic and Indian Oceans meet in a great swirl of currents, where Mary Kingsley's bones – I like to think – tumble this way and that on the sea floor amidst broken coral and sharks' teeth and the bones of shipwrecked sailors. Mon drove us up the steep hillside behind Rhodes's cottage on a so-called scenic road. We stopped beside a shark-spotting station, where two men, in radio contact with other stations further up the bay, were keeping a close eye on the water; by now I knew that this was absolutely not some kind of naturalists' shark-watching hobby. How could I ever have imagined swimming here? On the other side of the road a footpath snaked up the steep fynbos-purpled mountainside. A large sign warned hikers and cyclists to move only in large groups. Last month a man out hiking with his wife was stabbed to death, and only a couple of weeks ago a group of nine – nine! – hikers was attacked and robbed. Beneath the beauty of the mountain, as beneath the ocean's roll, lie danger, violence, death.

Down below us, next to Rhodes's cottage, we saw Randlord Abe Bailey's seaside house, where Elsie and John Kipling used to go and stay with the Bailey children, and over the sea road, almost on the beach, Bailey's cottage. Bailey's burial place was on the hillside just below us. Rhodes is buried in the rock of the Matopos Hills of Zimbabwe, the country that he stole from its inhabitants and which bore his name for nearly ninety years.

Returning to Cape Town, I misdirected Mon onto the wrong freeway. I must seriously reassess, in a downwards direction, my navigational or map-reading skills. It was quite hairy for both of us. Cape Town is literally the end of the road: all these freeways pour into it, and then the land just stops. Downtown is littered with unfinished roads: freeways stop in mid-air, pylons hold up empty traffic lanes going nowhere above the mess that is left of District Six, the historic dockside inner city of Cape Town, which in the 1960s and '70s was bulldozed into wreckage to make sure its black and coloured residents could never return.

15 February
Jacob Zuma has resigned.

Tanya has spent considerable time over the last couple of days ringing people up so as to make arrangements for us – me, Mon and Heinz – to go on a guided tour of Cecil Rhodes's house, Groote Schuur, which he left to the nation for a prime ministerial or presidential residence. The house is in Rondebosch, looking up to the Devil's Peak, and in the days when Rudyard and Carrie Kipling dined there with Rhodes, it was surrounded by gardens ablaze with colour and had a menagerie that included lions on the far side of the hibiscus and plumbago hedges. The gardens are now dry and dusty; the menagerie has long since vanished. The house itself, originally a seventeenth-century barn or granary built by the Dutch East India Company, was rebuilt for Rhodes by Herbert Baker, who later designed the Woolsack where the Kiplings spent many happy South African summers. When I was here three years ago I was reading a hilariously funny novel by Ann Harries called *Manly Pursuits*, which is all about the shenanigans of Rhodes and his favoured young men – along with the Kiplings and their mutual friend Dr Jameson – in Groote Schuur.

The tour guide, a smart young woman from Paarl, was informative and engaging. The tour lasted a whole two hours and cost only R50 each. Besides us there were a white South African couple and two elderly Frenchmen. And that was all. We saw some amazing furniture: some pieces designed by the talented Baker and some museum-quality pieces brought from here and there. I hadn't known that Hendrik Verwoerd, the Nazi-loving architect of apartheid, had been assassinated in Parliament, and by a knife-wielding man from Mozambique, no less. Nor did I know (why would I have known?) that Mrs de Klerk, who, the guide told us, was frightened the whole time she lived in Groote Schuur with her husband F. W. de Klerk that she would be murdered by an intruder coming in through the secret escape route in the bedroom (the entrance to which the guide showed us) that had been put in when the white government of the 1960s feared a black insurrection, had indeed actually been murdered...but not in Groote Schuur! After she and de Klerk divorced she moved into a flat in a gated (of course) luxury apartment block, and was murdered there.

When, in his will, Rhodes left Groote Schuur to the nation as a residence for future prime ministers, would he, or Kipling, have even imagined that such an office would one day have black incumbents? I don't think so.

After Rhodes's death, Kipling continued to bring his family out to Cape Town every winter to stay in the Woolsack, the house Rhodes had had built for him on the Groote Schuur estate. But Kipling's bitterness towards the Boers only increased when the Treaty of Vereeniging brought the war to an end in 1902; the granting of self-government to the Boer Republics in 1907, a mere five years later, was the final straw. The Kiplings left Cape Town for the last time in April 1908, and Rudyard never returned. I think it became a place of loss for him – the loss of his imperial dreams and the vision he had shared with Rhodes – and so it was too painful to go back, just as he never went back to America after the death there of his adored small daughter.

Years later, in 1928, Arthur Conan Doyle returned to South Africa, and wrote up the trip in a slim volume called *Our African Winter*. He was accompanied by his second wife Jean and their three children, and, after delivering a series of lectures on the importance of spiritualism (not as well received as he had hoped), he took the family to Bloemfontein where, nearly thirty years earlier, he had experienced the horrors of the typhoid epidemic that ravaged the British and imperial soldiers worse than anything on the battlefields. The Doyles were taken out of town by their hosts to visit the memorial (which I saw three years ago) to the 26,000 Boer women and children who had died in the British concentration camps. It seems it took Doyle a while to realize that not only was this not a commemoration of Boer fighting bravery (he viewed the Boer enemy in a very different light from Kipling), but that the words on the monument blamed the British for all the tens of thousands of civilian deaths. He was utterly affronted.

Self-esteem was restored over the border in Rhodesia, where the audiences showed more enthusiasm for the spiritualist message, and where Doyle visited Rhodes's grave in the Matopos Hills and, with the help of his wife's very own spirit guide, discussed with him matters of great pith and moment. He didn't publish his whole exchange with Rhodes's spirit because apparently it was too 'kindly' about Doyle himself and his work, but he published some excerpts from it as an appendix to *Our African Winter*. In their vagueness and generalizations the snippets of this exchange strike me as weirdly similar to Kipling's effusions on Rhodes after his death. Rhodes's ghost seems to have had a deadening effect on poetry and prose alike.

17 February

Mon and I decided we must take an Uber to the airport – to the relief, I do believe, of Tanya and Heinz. Whatever Heinz says about wanting and liking to drive, I think he nonetheless finds the airport road a challenge. And who wouldn't? Our Uber driver was from the Eastern Cape. Once a fortnight he does the twelve-hour drive home to see his family, a drive that is strange and scary. He told us that kudu – huge-shouldered antelope with long corkscrew horns – are strangely attracted by headlights, and rush onto the road and run straight at them. One crashed through the windscreen of a crowded minibus taxi and then struggled and kicked its way down the inside of the van and out of the back door, leaving every single passenger dead. An apocryphal story? I'm ready to believe anything.

Chapter 8

*February – July 2018; Ilminster, London, Home,
Bristol, Oxford*

23 February 2018

I have now been back from South Africa for a week, and once more
my shoulders are aching in the cold. An arctic wind howls around
the house. I can hardly believe that a week ago I was so hot I had to
sleep on top of the bedclothes.

Today I drove to Ilminster to meet Ken Cooper, editor and
publisher of *Aide-de-Camp to Conan Doyle: The Boer War Diary of
Charles Blasson*, which I came across while trawling around the
internet. Blasson, Ken's great-uncle by marriage, was a medical
student at University College Hospital and in 1900, aged twenty-
two, volunteered with four other students as a 'dresser' with
Langman's Field Hospital. He kept a journal in a notebook which
Ken found in a battered attaché case that had moved with him and
his wife, unopened, from attic to attic, through three house moves.
When Ken first opened the notebook he had no idea what he would
find, and was amazed to see the name 'Dr Conan Doyle'.

The journal covers the voyage out to South Africa and the
two months Blasson spent working with Doyle in the bell tents
of the field hospital that were set up on the cricket ground of the
Ramblers Club in Bloemfontein, the address of which Doyle and
his colleagues gave as 'Café Enterique, Boulevard des Microbes'.
Thousands of typhoid patients passed through those tents, or died

in them. Blasson grew close to Doyle, whom he looked up to as a father figure (he had recently lost his own father). Doyle employed him in his spare time to make fair copies of every chapter, as he completed them, of his history of the war, and to post them off to England. And Blasson was keeping his own account, jotting down notes in rough and then writing them up when he could.

As the field hospital moved by rail from Bloemfontein up to Pretoria in July 1900 (by which time Doyle was on board ship, homeward bound), Blasson continued to make rough notes for his journal. Did he realize that he too was coming down with typhoid? If he did, he didn't write about his suspicions or his fears. Ken told me he found it frustrating that Blasson didn't write about his feelings at all. When he said that, I realized that I sort of hadn't noticed. Perhaps because I wouldn't expect Blasson to write about his feelings: after all, none of the other men in my book write about theirs – well, not really, although Kipling of course mines them for his stories, and while Doyle sometimes can't contain an emotional outburst he's not exactly self-reflective. Blasson's journal is full of high spirits. He tells us about the japes he and the other medical dressers got up to when they weren't at work in the field hospital: chicken hunts, races on borrowed or stolen ponies, late-night practical jokes. He reminds me of Kipling's Stalky, or of Richmal Crompton's William: schoolboyish, innocent, uncomplicated. Or, alternatively, Blasson was suppressing his feelings, like so many men did then, and do now.

Blasson didn't have time to make a fair copy of the rough notes he made on the train ride from Bloemfontein to Pretoria. He died two days after the field hospital reached Pretoria, on his twenty-third birthday. By then Doyle was sailing home on the SS *Briton* (which was freshly painted in the new livery of the Union-Castle Line, with a lavender hull and red funnels topped in black), and hugely enjoying himself. He engaged in a lengthy quarrel with a pro-Boer Frenchman who accused the British of using the banned dumdum bullets (those damned dumdums: they seem to haunt this story); he listened closely to the spooky tales about the bleak and desolate moors of Devon and Cornwall recounted by one of his fellow passengers, the journalist Fletcher Robinson of *The Daily Express*. Back home, the two men would work together (initially) on the story that became *The Hound of the Baskervilles*, in which Sherlock Holmes would reappear before his public after an absence of seven years.

On disembarkation, Doyle hurried to London to meet up with his dearest mother (of course), and, from Morley's Hotel in Trafalgar Square where they had taken rooms, he wrote to Blasson's mother, giving her the conventional line about noble sacrifice in the service of his country. He also told her – and I'm sure not all senior officers did this – how fond he had been of her son. I like him for that. Ken has included a photograph of the letter in an appendix to the diary.

As I was saying goodbye, Ken pressed two books on me: Brian Pugh's Conan Doyle chronology, and a handsome British Library facsimile edition of Doyle's 1880 Arctic diary.

28 February

The dog's water bowl was frozen solid this morning, and a stalagmite had formed in the sink beneath the scullery tap. Thank God I brought her bed into the warm kitchen last night. My knuckles are raw, and bleed when the skin cracks open. Typing is painful. But the sun is shining in a clear blue sky. I've been working on various ideas for the lecture that lovely Julia – who invited me to the A Suitcase of Her Own conference – has asked me to give at the University of Silesia.

I have been reading Olive Schreiner's *From Man to Man*. The prelude, titled 'A Child's Day', recounts the day on which five-year-old Rebekah's baby sister Bertie (a surviving twin) is born. It is Woolfian in the intense interiority of Rebekah's passions, fantasies, fears. Will she ever live so intensely again? Schreiner never finished the novel. She was writing it for over forty years! What a pity she had no editor to snatch it from her hands and force her to sit down and shape it into a final form. The fall of Bertie reminds me of the fall of Lily Bart in *The House of Mirth*. These strong-willed, passionate heroines! The Victorian patriarchy just couldn't cope with them.

Kipling first met Schreiner when she was already famous as the author of *The Story of an African Farm*, which was published in 1883, and before she wrote *Trooper Peter Halket of Mashonaland*, her fierce critique of Rhodes's violent imperialism, a novel which lost her many friends. Kipling went to visit her on his first trip to South Africa in 1891, when he was twenty-five years old and voyaging round the world to escape from the depression and madness he had fallen into in London. She was living 500 miles north of Cape Town, in Matjiesfontein, struggling with her asthma and all her other worries. By all accounts they got on well and enjoyed long writerly conversations. *Trooper Peter Halket* was published in England by T. Fisher Unwin in 1897. When I borrowed it from the Bristol University library I was amazed to find that I had in my hands Jane Cobden Unwin's own copy, inscribed to her by her husband, the publisher. I was even more amazed – shocked, even – when I lifted up the tissue guard protecting the frontispiece, and found a photograph of a lynching: a semicircle of seven grinning white men standing round a tree, from whose branches dangled three black bodies. That was the kind of racial violence Schreiner was attacking.

Schreiner had met Cecil Rhodes at Kimberley when they were both very young, and the diamonds had only just been discovered and it was all up for grabs, for black as well as for white prospectors.

She had liked him then. But he had consolidated his power and turned the mine into an efficient profit-making machine on the backs of black labourers, and then he had seized Matabeleland. Schreiner would no longer speak to him; indeed, encountering him by chance on a railway platform, she turned her back on him. When she and her husband Cron sailed to England with the manuscript of *Trooper Peter Halket*, taking it to Unwin in London, Rhodes was a fellow passenger. According to William Plomer's elegantly hostile biography, Rhodes sent his manservant to break into their cabin and find the manuscript. And destroy it? Plomer doesn't say. The ploy was unsuccessful, presumably because Schreiner was highly suspicious, and knew that Rhodes was furious about her novel and its picture of his murderous activities in Matabeleland.

When I reread *The Story of an African Farm*, I was struck by the parallels between the situation of the young farm boy Waldo and that of poor little Punch in Kipling's autobiographical story 'Baa Baa Black Sheep'. Both boys are bullied and cruelly abused in the name of religious morality; both are comforted by a younger girl-child, just as in real life Rudyard was comforted by his little sister Trix when he was being punished by the cruel woman in whose care the two children had been left.

The friendship between Schreiner and Kipling did not survive the outbreak of the Boer War, in which they found themselves on opposing sides.

1 March

The first day of spring has blown in on the wings of a biting cold wind so penetrating that I was actually forced to turn back from this morning's walk across the fields. I noticed how even a bare hedge provides a windbreak. You just have to look at how the sheep are huddled and you know that they know that too. But walking across the big field, there are no hedges anywhere near to provide even a tiny bit of shelter. The blizzard is due in at 3pm.

I am thinking of including in my book a central chapter that will showcase the voices of others: people in South Africa who are caught up in the conflict before my three main subjects arrive there fresh from England. Players such as Olive Schreiner; Lieutenant Colonel Robert Kekewich, besieged in Kimberley; Solomon Plaatje, besieged in Mafeking; Mohandas Gandhi, who in Durban set up the Indian Ambulance Corps in the service of Britain and her empire; Roger Casement, lurking in Lourenço Marques; the journalist H. W. Nevinson, who was trapped in Ladysmith; John Tengo Jabavu, who edited a Xhosa/English-language newspaper in the Eastern Cape (Tanya put me on his track). Perhaps – if I can get hold of the material – even President Kruger. ('Sloven, sullen, savage, secret, uncontrolled,' according to Kipling in full warmongering mode in a poem printed in *The Times* twelve days before war was declared.) The ones who weren't keeping journals were busy writing letters (or telegrams in the case of Gandhi and Kruger).

7 March

I have been struggling for days over my lecture for the University of Silesia, and have just sent the current draft off to Michèle and Jenny prior to our Group of Three meeting next week, and also a copy to HB.

For the Suitcase conference I wrote my lecture – 'The Art of Rambling' – swiftly and easily, once I had discovered what and whom it was going to be about. This lecture is very different: I'm having to drag it out of myself. Although it starts with Conan Doyle's visit to Green Point POW camp, and my and Mon's – serendipitous – discovery of the site when we were in Cape Town, nonetheless it remains vague and abstract. It needs a shaping narrative, if not an actual argument.

12 March

I have recently been having a series of anxiety/failure dreams. In last night's dream I was dropped from a radio show by the producer, who was my former boss from the university. My goodness, how this dream comes around. How many years is it since I was dropped as presenter of *A Good Read*? At least fifteen! Last night's iteration was less about getting kicked out of my teaching without notice – the all-too-common fate of hourly paid tutors at the University of Bristol, and indeed probably all universities (an astonishing, disgraceful 25% of university teachers/lecturers are contracted as HPTs, HB recently told me, lacking all basic employment rights) – and more to do with deep anxiety about my book. I am feeling increasingly undermined by my agent's long silence. What does it mean?

17 March

Flurries of snow are drifting past the window as I write. I am fed up with the snow, bored by the eternal cold.

On Wednesday I cut my prednisolone dose by half a milligram. So I'm now taking 5.5, which is quite awkward as I have to take four pills: one 2.5 milligram and three 1 milligram. It would be good to get down to a single pill of 5 milligrams. I feel bloated at the moment. I need to exercise more. The pain is just about manageable.

I spent Monday in London in the Westminster Reference Library, reading Georgina Doyle's *Out of the Shadows*, her account of Conan Doyle's first family: his wife Touie (Louise Hawkins) and their two children, Mary and Kingsley. (Mary and Kingsley – for me a strange coincidence of names.) Georgina Doyle (now Lady

Wilson) is Doyle's niece by marriage: she was married to Innes's son. Innes was Arthur's only brother, fourteen years younger than him, who served in the Army throughout the First World War and then died in 1919 in the Spanish flu epidemic. *Out of the Shadows* was published some years ago in Canada by a small press that no longer exists. I could find trace of only two copies of it in this country: in Redland Library in Bristol, from which it has long been missing, and here in the Sherlock Holmes Collection in Westminster. The Reference Library is in 35 St Martin's Street, and was once upon a time the home of Isaac Newton. It is a stone's throw from the back of the National Gallery, where I met Michèle for a quick dash around the small but exquisitely beautiful Van Eyck/Pre-Raphaelite exhibition and a cup of tea. Back in the Reference Library, I was surrounded by old men snoozing over the *TLS*, young men taking photos of each other, and a hijab-wearing student eating her lunch, until a librarian asked her not to. Only one room was open (the rest were closed for refurbishment), so we were all crowded in together.

Georgina Doyle champions poor Touie (lingering death from TB) over Jean Leckie who, once she was safely married to Arthur, sought the limelight, waved her arms around too much, and was beastly to her stepchildren Mary and Kingsley. Mary was sent abroad – to Dresden – as soon as her father and Jean were married, and not allowed home, not even for Christmas. She and her brother were very close, and she missed him desperately. Doyle's failure to stand up for his and Touie's children against their stepmother lowers him in my esteem. Jean was fifteen years younger than him. There's no fool like an old fool but, alas, old fools are still capable of hurting others and inflicting damage.

By the time Kingsley died in 1918, aged twenty-five, Arthur, with Jean's encouragement, had become a committed spiritualist. He was lecturing on the subject on the evening he heard of his son's death. 'Had I not been a Spiritualist I could not have spoken that night. As it was, I was able to go straight on the platform and tell the meeting that I knew my son had survived the grave, and that there was no need to worry.'[6] By then he had three more children with Jean. Mary would be pretty much cut out of his will. He left all his literary copyrights to his second family. Mary hoped that she would at least inherit her own mother's jewellery, but by the time her father died it had mysteriously vanished.

The following day we had a sustaining Group of Three meeting. Jenny and Michèle had read my lecture with care and made some excellent suggestions, such as to cut down on the too many pages on Richard Holmes and his brilliance as a biographer. Almost at once it became clear to me – as I listened to Michèle and Jenny's comments – that I had written those pages as a displacement (yet again) for my anxiety about what I myself am saying in the lecture about the biographical process.

23 March

On Tuesday I sent my agent a curt email asking her what was going on. She hadn't even replied to my polite email of a fortnight ago asking when I might, please, expect to hear from her about the draft I sent at the end of January. She replied to this one by return, which just goes to show that, unfortunately, rudeness does get results. She said she would be in touch next week with her comments. But I am no longer interested in her comments. I emailed her again yesterday and asked why she couldn't send out my proposal now, immediately. No reply.

4 April

My agent was *not* in touch with me with her comments. Not in touch at all. I feel I don't have anything to lose… I emailed again

---

6   *Arthur Conan Doyle: A Life in Letters*, ed. by Jon Lellenberg et al., 2007, Harper Press, p. 648.

yesterday: why not pass my book on to one of her colleagues at the agency if she has no time to represent me herself, or, if that were not possible, let me know so that I could then decide what to do? I pointed out that she had promised to send out my proposal over a year ago. I am feeling desperate. All I want is for someone to say, 'Yes, we're interested.'

HB has put my illustrations for the Poland lecture into a PowerPoint slide presentation. The lecture is now called 'Empathy and Empty Spaces: Adventures in Life-Writing'. A fancy title often helps the thoughts run freer.

5 April

After three weeks of constant aching pain behind my breastbone, and fire in my shoulders, I have yielded and increased the steroid dose from 5.5 milligrams to 7.5. When will this end?

6 April

A reply from my agent! She *did* send out the proposal last year, and *did* tell me. Unfortunately, this flurry of activity took place during the six months when she was using – inexplicably – my long-defunct Hotmail address. Some people, I now discover, have already said that they are not interested: Bloomsbury, Icon, HarperCollins and Penguin have all passed on it.

21 April

My fellow RLF Fellow Julian Evans, who organizes the regional RLF Writing Project, rang in response to my email of a week or two ago in which I confessed to feeling paralysed by my agent's lack of activity on my behalf, and quite unable to carry out the Writing Project's agenda of making cold calls to companies to pitch workshops in writing skills. He said he completely understood. And then he said, why didn't I just ask the editor of my previous book if he'd like to have a look at my current book – and surely he would! Then he said that he, Julian, thinks that I write really good emails, and that of course my editor is going to respond at once to my query and then snap the book up. How very sweet of him to say all those things, how kind.

Has my agent been in touch with Michael Dwyer at Hurst? Somehow, I doubt it.

Meanwhile I had emailed my agent to let her know that tomorrow I would be in Cambridge – where she and her husband live – for Richard Gooder's memorial at Clare College, and could we perhaps meet for a drink? She didn't reply. Yesterday afternoon I thought, How rude not to even reply, so I sent a single line, saying, 'Drink? Yes or no? Please let me know.' She answered at once: yes. I'm meeting her at The Free Press after Richard's memorial.

2 May

When I met up with my agent at last, she was completely charming and said my book was wonderfully rich and what I must do now is write an introduction for the general reader (and general editor), and then once I've removed all the 'notes to self' that pepper the text she will send it all out. All my negative thoughts about her flew out the window; I felt massively encouraged.

19 May

When I last saw my brother James I described to him how, since the onset of PMR and my daily ingestion of prednisolone and lansoprazole (I switched to the latter when omeprazole made me feel utterly nauseous), I have been suffering from chronic diarrhoea. Lansoprazole (like omeprazole) is a proton pump inhibitor, and is meant to reduce the amount of acid in the stomach, which I *think* is increased by the steroids. The diarrhoea is almost, but not quite, a daily occurrence. It strikes apparently randomly, although invariably at times of stress. I mean it comes on worse than usual when it is stress-related: on the South Africa trip, the Poland trip, any public appearance at all, any aeroplane flight, any train journey, any long drive... James said, 'Well, many GPs are ignorant of two common side effects of lansoprazole: heart arrhythmia, and... chronic diarrhoea.' It can cause what James called 'micro colitis'.

Since our conversation I have stopped taking it, and I would say my bowels are definitely steadier. The night-time acid reflux, however, has returned, so I'm taking two Gaviscon tablets when I go to bed, and another one in the middle of the night if I need to. Which makes me feel very *chalky* in the morning. But feeling chalky is considerably preferable to having uncontrollable watery diarrhoea. I cannot believe that none of the many GPs I have consulted over the last two years have thought to mention this side effect. Indeed, some of them were insistent that I take the horrible alendronic acid as well which, as any fule kno, does no bloody good at all unless you actually suffer from osteoporosis, which I don't, and in fact is more likely to poison me than anything else. This whole system – GPs prescribing one pill after another, so that the patient ends up ill and debilitated as a result – lies at the heart of James's new book, *Too Many Pills*. Yes, indeed, too many pills.

I have now carefully studied the information leaflet that comes with the lansoprazole (which I obviously should have done two years ago). In summary: 1) if diarrhoea occurs, contact your doctor immediately; 2) common side effects (i.e. occurring in more than one in 100 patients) include diarrhoea (so presumably *don't* contact your doctor immediately?); and 3) very rare side effects (less than one in 10,000 patients) include colitis, or inflammation of the bowel. Hmm. Clear as mud.

Meanwhile I've been on 6.5 milligrams of prednisolone since last week, down from 7 milligrams. The level of pain varies daily. Constant pain in the sternum. James has suggested I might try a non-steroidal anti-inflammatory, but the possibility of developing giant cell arteritis without the steroid protection, and thereby putting myself in danger of sudden and irreversible blindness, is too frightening.

19 June

After two unanswered emails from me, the agent wrote on Friday, 'I am submitting…', which leads me to suspect that she hasn't actually done so yet, or she would have written, 'I have submitted…' Still, an inch forward. But she's away all this week, so maybe nothing will be sent out until next week. It would be good if you could track your agent's submissions, as you can track an Amazon parcel.

26 June

I went to London on the hottest day of the year to meet Julia and Zbigniew, who are over from the University of Silesia for a conference at King's College, and to visit the Royal Academy summer exhibition, which I always love and which this year is curated by Grayson Perry. My sister-in-law Dolores, who works in the RA learning department, took us round and was wonderfully informative; then she took the three of us to the grand Senate Room bar in the newly opened back section of Burlington House. We ordered a bottle of Sancerre and I talked about how anxious I was about my book; how not knowing if anyone would want it was filling me with dread; how I didn't know what to do next. 'Send it immediately to your last editor,' advised Zbigniew. He said he couldn't imagine not sending a new book to a previous editor. That was what he always did. And I shouldn't be nervous about it. He made it all sound perfectly reasonable. I am aware that this is what Julian Evans suggested I do two months ago. Why haven't I? I think perhaps it's because now that I actually have an agent – however silent and invisible – I can't bear the idea of receiving a direct rejection. Is that it? Or is it that I am actually scared of, or subservient to, said agent?

I have just emailed Michael Dwyer at Hurst to ask if my book has actually been submitted to him for consideration...

7 July

Michael replied by return: no, it hasn't been, and yes, he would love to read it. I have sent it.

Since then I have been mopping my brow in the Central Reference Library in Bristol where I've been looking at the 1900 issues of *The Illustrated London News, The Graphic* and *Black & White*, a few of which I rattled through in the National Library of South Africa in Cape Town. It is moderately cool down the corridor in the computer area, but here in the reading room we have no fans, nor any air conditioning. I am the only person here save for two wild-bearded old men slumped over newspapers. The librarians willingly wheel the extremely heavy bound folio volumes of the magazines in and out for me on a heavy-duty wheelie truck. The 'pencils only' rule, laid down by almost every archive I've worked in, is not practised here (well, I guess it's not an archive, but they do hold some pretty old and valuable stuff); nor is there any problem with me snapping away with my phone. And why should there be? Everything I want is out of copyright.

They were very nervous indeed about the taking of photos in the NLSA (and in the Special Collections at the University of Cape Town, too). Things that happened in South Africa even at the very beginning of the twentieth century remain alive; they are still contentious, still dangerous. I have found the issue of *Black & White* that I saw in Cape Town, with the cover sketch of Solomon Plaatje acting as interpreter while two 'natives' are interrogated by white men in the magistrates' court in Mafeking. Images of Plaatje in Mafeking are very rare. I saw this one in the NLSA and tried to secretly take a photo of it, after I'd been told I wasn't allowed to take any photos at all. My hand was shaking so much that the photo came out blurred.

The magazines are stuffed with war artists' sketches of cadaverous horses abandoned on the veldt, heads lowered, waiting for the end, encircled by evil-eyed vultures; and of British soldiers fighting vultures off their half-dead horses with the butts of their rifles. These sketches have captions like 'Dismissed the Army' or 'His Faithful Friend'. In *Towards Pretoria* the journalist Julian Ralph, one of Kipling's co-editors on *The Friend*, described the greedy *aasvogels* waiting for the starving horses abandoned by the British troops to drop dead, or to become too weak to fight them off. According to Thomas Pakenham over 400,000 horses, donkeys and mules were 'expended', in the weasel word of the War Office, during the course of the war. The troops were under strict instruction to leave their wounded and dying mounts on the battlefields, so as not to make themselves targets for Boer snipers, but many of the men crept back under cover of darkness to put an end to their horses' suffering.

On Tuesday I'm off to Oxford for two days to look at Alice Stopford Green's letters to John Holt in the Bodleian, and as many as I can track down of the ninety-one – ninety-one! – objects bequeathed by Mary Kingsley to the Pitt Rivers Museum, including a nail-studded, blood-strengthened *Mavungu*, which – or rather who – is on public display.

10 July
Wadham College, Oxford, staircase 24, room 12. I have been given a room up at the top of the building, unlike last time I was here, two years ago, when I was given a boiling hot ground-floor room with windows onto the street, which of course couldn't be left open. Now I have opened all my windows wide and I can even climb out

onto a flat roof and look out across the crowding, spired, slanting roofs towards the dome of the Ashmolean. It looks like the Oxford of Jordan College in *His Dark Materials*.

It took two trains and a bus (the latter from Didcot) to get here this morning, but I was in the Bodleian soonish after midday. I read Alice Stopford Green's letter to John Holt about the conditions of the exiled Boer POWs on St Helena, and I've looked at some of the Holt/E. D. Morel correspondence. When I was here two years ago I had no idea that this material was so interesting. I am not sure I even knew that it existed.

11 July

Over breakfast at the long tables in Wadham dining hall (piles of fresh fruit, excellent free-range scrambled eggs) I eavesdropped on a conversation between the two men next to me, an Australian of about sixty, and, opposite him, a slightly younger Dutch man. They were discussing Brexit. The Dutch man expressed pity for the British people being taken in by a bunch of privileged Etonians. The Australian said that in Australia a referendum is considered valid only if 70% vote for it: otherwise it is seen as too divisive. Then they discussed the beautiful old architecture of Eastern Europe. The Dutch man said he went to Leipzig during the Cold War to do some research on Bach. Recently he was back there and, after seeing the German film *The Lives of Others* (about people spying on each other in East Germany), he thought he would have a look at the secret police files to see if by any chance his name cropped up anywhere. He didn't really expect it to. But yes: every single trivial exchange he had had – with the sales assistant in a bookshop; with a waiter in a café – had been reported and recorded. It takes a long time for people to get over that, he said; not just those spied upon, but those doing the spying.

12 July

Michael Dwyer at Hurst has said he would love to publish my book. Those were his words: 'love to'. I can hardly believe it.

Chapter 9

*July – December 2018; Home, Brighton, Home,
Rottingdean, Home*

18 July 2018

I realize now that I could have sent the manuscript to Michael
Dwyer six months ago, when I had completed a draft and rewritten
the proposal and chapter breakdown. Thus I would have avoided
six months of waiting and waiting, and feebly not daring to email
my agent, and falling into a trough of despair. But that seems to
be my way.

Michael has not yet forwarded the comments from his
in-house reader; I am having to remind myself every day that there
must be some other reason for the delay than that he's changed
his mind about publishing the book… Meanwhile I am going to
put away the Mary Kingsley/Alice Stopford Green material I have
recently been thinking about, and focus instead on preparing to
go over to the University of Sussex to look at the Kipling Papers,
which are in the university's archives in a place called The Keep,
written in lower case with square brackets: '[the keep]'; also to visit
Rottingdean on the coast, where the Kiplings lived for a few years
before the Boer War, and Bateman's, the house they bought in 1902
and where they lived thereafter.

21 July

Michael sent me the comments on my book from his in-house

editor/reader. How interesting it is to get someone else's view, for the very first time, on what they think I am doing or not doing with the material. The reader's 'only reservation': 'just because these writers were using the continent and the war as a dumping-ground for their personal emotional baggage doesn't mean that the author should necessarily allow that framework to dictate her writing about the conflict', and the reader would like some acknowledgement of that framework when I write the prologue. Yet this is precisely my interpretation: the 'something' of themselves that sent my subjects out to the war in South Africa. And, the three of them embodying as they did various different aspects of end-of-the-century British imperialism, they provide the principal perspectives through which I look at how that imperialist war was waged.

Michael also sent a brief note – he's on holiday – saying something about how things will depend on 'your agent's expectations', which makes me think that, despite all indications to the contrary, my agent actually *has* been in touch with him – in a sinister fashion! I'll ask him what he means next week when he's back in the office; for the moment I shall try not to fret.

26 July

I spoke to Michael on the phone this morning. He finds my prose 'pleasing'. Oh, how I love this man! He will sell the book to Oxford University Press (OUP) in the USA – or, if not, get them to distribute the Hurst edition – and to one of the South African houses. He told me the Hurst office has a new gang of keen young editors and publicists; that the book can be illustrated with photos and maps; and when I said that the narrative structure which his reader wished me to acknowledge was, in fact, invented by me, Michael said that the reader's response showed the clarity and success of my structure, and that that was something to be proud of.

I have written a polite farewell email to my agent. Just before I sent it I thought that perhaps I should quickly check the agency website to see what it said about me. My name does not appear on her client list. There is nothing about me, nor my book. After two whole years, for crying out loud!

Who cares? Now I have a publisher who finds my writing pleasing. On with the rewrite!

30 July

I have put a countersigned contract in the post to Michael, sent him some draft catalogue copy, discussed the wording of the title, and made some suggestions for cover images. The title I am going for, with a nod to Rudyard Kipling's reticent memoir *Something of Myself,* is *Something of Themselves.* My earlier working title, *Escape to Africa,* smacks too much of Haggard and Henty and end-of-empire adventure fantasies. While my argument is precisely that at least two of my subjects *did* indulge those fantasies regarding the war in South Africa, the last thing I want is for the book itself to be seen to subscribe to them, when in fact what I'm hoping it does is provide an analysis – or, if not an analysis, at least a series of pictures – of the crumbling of empire in the fiasco of that war.

Meanwhile the agent has replied, politely, apologizing for her tardiness over the last few months (hmm: years, I'd say), and telling me that, due to her full schedule, she had actually been on the point of relieving herself of me anyway, and passing me on to someone else in the agency. So now she won't even have to do that. Good outcome all round: no tears shed, nor angry emails exchanged.

10 August

I spent hours yesterday trying to check the date of William Strang's etching of Kipling, which, to me, shows grief marked deeply on his face; the desperate grief, I assumed, that followed the death of his small daughter Josephine in New York in March 1899 while he himself was hovering – unconscious – between life and death. Renée Durbach dates the picture to 1899, but my research kept on turning up 1897 or 1898: in other words, *before* Josephine died.

I have managed to revise the first two Kipling chapters, but then I was distracted from Kipling by an exchange of emails with the Irish historian Angus Mitchell on the subject of Roger Casement, Alice Stopford Green, and the Holt Papers in the Bodleian. Mitchell is the author of a lively and sympathetic biography of Casement in the O'Brien Press's 16 Lives series ('Sixteen lives that changed the course of Irish History'), being biographies of the sixteen men executed after the 1916 Easter Rising. He has also done a lot of research on the lovely Alice, and has produced a typescript of the journal of her voyage to St Helena in 1900 to investigate the conditions of the exiled Boer POWs. He has been extremely helpful, digging out his old notes and references, many of which he made back when all the Holt material on Africa was kept in Rhodes House, before it was moved over the road into the Bodleian's new Weston Library.

When the Boers declared war in October 1899, Casement left his consular post in the Congo and Angola for Lourenço Marques in Portuguese East Africa (as Mozambique was then called), in order to spy out and report back to London on the quantity and type of arms flowing west towards Pretoria, capital of the Transvaal. Casement is going to be one of the voices from South Africa in chapter 7.

13 August

I left home at 1pm today and arrived in Brighton just before six. I had to change trains three times – at Bristol Temple Meads, Reading and Gatwick – and in between each change I fell into a slumber; then I walked what seemed like miles to the Topps Hotel in Regency Square. I think by mistake I took an especially long route to it. I was exhausted, but knew I'd feel better after something to eat and drink, so I went out immediately to find a pub. I'm always a bit apprehensive going into a strange pub on my own, so once I find a nice, comfortable one – such as The Slaughter House in Liverpool – I stick with it. Turning towards the town centre, the first pub I found had sour beer, a sour-faced barman, and no food on a Monday. I retraced my steps to Regency Square, went beyond it westwards, and braved a different pub, in a street filled with Thai, Chinese and Korean eateries and stores, where I had a tasty red Thai curry and drank a Belgian wheat beer. The proprietor of the Topps Hotel is Chinese, possibly Hong Kong Chinese. The whole area reminds me of Vancouver: what with the sea visible at the end of the road, it all feels a bit Pacific Rim. A young Chinese woman was ordered to carry my suitcase up the two flights of stairs to my room, which is spare, basic, clean, and overlooks the street where I had my supper. Now that I am fed, watered and showered I feel a million times better, and strong enough to find The Keep (or [the keep]) tomorrow and face all the Kipling material it holds.

14 August

Why, oh why did I not think to take a packed lunch with me to [the keep], which is already in my bad books for its stupid modern – or maybe postmodern – logo with its silly lower-case letters and silly square brackets? The unexceptional building is in the middle of a forest seemingly miles from anywhere, and the only refreshments on offer are crisps and sweets from one vending machine and instant coffee from another. Nothing else. Not even pre-packed sandwiches. I asked the woman at the desk where was the closest place to buy a sandwich. She sucked her teeth for half a minute and said, doubtfully, 'The campus?'

'And how far away is the campus?'

'Fifteen minutes.'

Jeez. Why couldn't they say on the website, 'although we are an internationally renowned institution holding the archives of the University of Sussex and the whole of Sussex County, you can't buy a sandwich here or get a decent hot drink, so make sure to bring your own'?

The archivists appear to be in the process of re-cataloguing the items in the Kipling Papers. The only way you can order is via the creaky online catalogue: there are no paper order slips, no pencils. [the keep] is much too modern for such old-fashioned tools. Each time you want to order something you have to log in online, and after you've ordered you have to wait for at least fifteen minutes. I ordered – randomly – one of the files I thought might be of interest, and the woman who handed it over to me said, 'Well, I've got the whole box in the back room, so perhaps you could look through it rather than order up each file in turn.' She must realize that their official system drives people crazy. I still have to look at each file separately and in turn, but at least I'm avoiding the fifteen-minute waits in between. It wouldn't be so bad if you knew beforehand what was in each file and what you wanted to read, but of course, and as always, most of us do not know. That is why we are here.

I looked at material relating to the death of six-year-old Josephine Kipling in New York at the beginning of March 1899. Her father Rudyard had double pneumonia and was dicing with death himself; Josephine came down with pneumonia after he did and then she developed dysentery. She died while he was still in a coma; he hadn't even known she was ill. I read two letters from Alice Kipling, Rudyard's mother, to her sister Georgiana Burne-Jones: she expresses coldness towards if not downright dislike of her daughter-in-law Carrie; in one letter she cannot even write Carrie's name, but refers to her throughout as 'she', a manifest sign of hostility; in the other she blames Carrie for Josephine's death, for having sent the children out for walks in wintry New York. Alice at the time was coping with Rudyard's mentally ill sister Trix, who was in the middle of one of her bouts of alternating mutism and mania. But even so, how cold and unkind she was to Carrie. In New York Carrie got her and Rudyard's friend Frank Doubleday to write to Rudyard's agent A. P. Watt to tell him what had happened, saying that she herself could not bear to ever speak of it again, and to ask him, Watt, to pass on her account of the child's death to Rudyard's parents.

When Josephine fell ill, a few days after her father, Carrie had sent her across Manhattan to the house of an old friend of theirs, to be nursed there. Early in the morning of 6 March, Carrie heard that her daughter had died; she was in the Hotel Grenoble, on call for Rudyard who had himself just stepped back from the brink of death but was still feverish and unconscious. Poor little Josephine, six years old, dying alone, with neither mother nor father beside her. Poor Carrie, unable to tell Rudyard that his daughter was dead in case it sent him into a fatal relapse. She had to carry the whole grievous burden alone.

At lunchtime I sat on one of the walls in the concreted space outside the building and chatted with a guy from the University of Southampton. He is writing a book on the pensions and compensations paid to wounded soldiers and their widows after the English Civil War. He has already published one book which focuses on people from Devon; now he's going nationwide. Many of the claims and testimonies are in Latin, he said, and of course in strange old seventeenth-century handwriting. Rather him than me. We shared a moan about the lack of refreshments, the lack of benches to sit on outside, and the lack of a pleasant prospect. He had brought his own sandwiches. I ate a bag of crisps.

At closing time I asked if I could mark some files to be set aside for me to look at tomorrow, as is common archival practice, so that I wouldn't have to reorder in the morning. No, I was told: everything goes back to the repository overnight, and has to be ordered again online in the morning. Aargh!

15 August

This morning, planning to be at The Keep by what I thought was opening time at 9.30, I climbed aboard the bus that takes you to the university campus, but got off again when the driver told me that they didn't stop at The Keep. How strange, I thought: a university bus that doesn't stop at the library. The buses here are named after local writers and other notables; it's rather sweet. I've seen one called 'Angela Thirkell'. She was the daughter of Rudyard Kipling's cousin Margaret, and wrote a lovely memoir – called *Three Houses* – about her childhood, and happy summer days with Josephine in Rottingdean. I had to wait for another bus, and was feeling pissed off with myself because I would lose half an hour of reading time. But as it turned out, The Keep doesn't open until 10am, despite it saying 9.30 on the online order forms.

I realize now that the lines around 'the keep' are not square brackets. They look like brackets but they don't have feet to them. Thus, the vertical lines with the little overhang at the top look like – or indeed represent or symbolize – a castle or, indeed, a keep! OK, my mistake! I remain irritated by it nonetheless.

Today I read more letters of condolence received by Carrie Kipling in the days following Josephine's death. Generous, affectionate Aunt Georgie Burne-Jones assures Carrie that she'll keep an eye on the house and garden for her for as long as she and Rudyard are away from home. There is nothing at all – not a peep – from Carrie's mother-in-law Alice; a struggling letter from Lockwood, Carrie's father-in-law, saying that he doesn't know what to say about the loss of 'our Josephine', though he then goes on to say it at some length; lots of press cuttings. The death was announced to the press that night, and was reported alongside a notice that physicians had given warning that the news of it might prove a fatal shock to Josephine's father.

When Rudyard regained consciousness on the morning of 6 March, Carrie greeted him, according to press reports, with 'a reassuring smile'. She had heard only two or three hours earlier that their child had just died. How could she ever forgive her husband for the tragedy? Perhaps that was why it was never spoken of again to anyone else, and probably not between them either: her rage, I speculate, was profound. Henry James used the word 'sacrifice' to describe the death of Josephine. 'Dear little vanished delightful Josephine,' he wrote to Carrie; 'dear little surrendered sacrificed soul!' The father lived; the daughter died. The daughter died in order that the father might live. The first child was sacrificed to Rudyard for his life; the second child, their son John, sacrificed (in this instance my word, not James's) to Rudyard's notions of England and empire. How could Carrie not have hated him? Was that why, ultimately, she became so fierce a keeper of the flame? Having lost her two favourite children, perhaps she needed to devote the rest of her life and energies to ensuring that the sacrifice was worthwhile? I know that it was not Kipling's fault that he caught double pneumonia and nearly died; not his fault that his daughter also fell ill and did die; nonetheless, for the last two days I have been feeling an increasing dislike of him.

After I got back to the hotel I went out for a walk along the deserted pebble beach towards the burned-out West Pier, and came across an attractive-looking glass-walled bar/restaurant with, as I could see through the glass, only one customer inside. A woman on her own; always a good sign. I went in and ordered a glass of wine, and then HB, on the phone, said, why didn't I stay and have something to eat there? I thought, Why not? So here I am, safely settled by the sea (the English Channel, granted, rather than the

Pacific Ocean), a ghostly row of wind turbines on the horizon, waves breaking on the shingle to either side of the ruined West Pier, and a windsurfer beneath a multicoloured sail foaming through the now-grey waves. The other solitary woman has departed, but two other women have appeared, and are busy discussing daughters, husbands, houses, lovers...

20 August

I haven't yet processed any of last week's research, or indeed quite finished typing up my notes, and I have had a couple of bad insomniac nights. I hardly ever suffer from insomnia: I think it must be because of all the stuff swirling round in my head, unprocessed and disordered.

I started reading and am now halfway through Angus Wilson's *The Strange Ride of Rudyard Kipling*, which unsurprisingly is very good indeed, wonderfully writerly, and I should have read it months ago, but better late...

21 August

Through the good offices of my (former) ELCE teaching colleague Sandra Hopkins and her husband David, who is a professor of English, their friend Daniel Karlin has kindly offered to read and comment on my Kipling chapters. Karlin is Winterstoke Professor of Literature at Bristol, and has edited, and written scholarly introductions to, various anthologies of Kipling's prose and poetry. He recently wrote a brilliant essay in *The Kipling Journal* on the subtleties of the language used by Boots and his friends in *Thy Servant a Dog*, a book I absolutely adore.

3 September

I am about to read through my reworked chapter 9 (Kipling in Cape Town and Bloemfontein). It has taken me six – *six* – weeks to revise three Kipling chapters! I did have time off from actual writing while I was over at The Keep, but even so!

7 September

The autumn term begins. I bumped into RDA organizer Lucy in Yatton post office last week, and she said that as the first-session children (who all come from the same school) aren't able to come to RDA next week, how about all the volunteers meet for coffee, biscuits and catch-up at Little Grange before the second session? Good idea, I said.

Nicky had spent the summer looking after her cat, who is on steroids and has to be on a respirator twice a day. Twice! How on earth...? 'With difficulty,' said Nicky. I told her about Ismay and me attempting to get Skitty into the cat basket that wasn't really a cat basket but a top-opening picnic hamper, in order to take her to the vet. And how, just like a cartoon cat, she stuck all four legs out rigid on either side of her so that she couldn't be lowered in, before wriggling out of our grasp and scarpering.

Hilary said she had read the introduction and the first two chapters of *Rose Macaulay*, and that it was like reading a novel. She felt she was there, in Italy, with the Macaulay children. It was all so readable, she said, including the introduction, that it drew her on. I told her I was struggling with the introduction to the new book. What she said made me think about how I must try to spin a story in it. Thank you, Hilary.

Gill had baked a lemon cake. I provided some chocolate biscuits. I didn't stay for the actual riding session because I still hadn't finished making the changes to my final Kipling chapter, so I rushed home, made the changes, printed out all the Kipling chapters and put them in a Jiffy bag along with the introduction and summaries of the in-between (i.e. Mary Kingsley and Arthur Conan Doyle) chapters, and sent them all off to Daniel Karlin.

Phew! I then hoovered the house top to bottom and cleaned the sitting-room windows.

16 September

Rottingdean on the East Sussex coast, a mile or two east of Brighton: Kipling first saw The Elms when he was sixteen and staying in Rottingdean with Uncle Ned and Aunt Georgie Burne-Jones in North End House, their holiday home, before he sailed to India to begin his 'seven years hard' of journalism. The Elms was across the village green from the Burne-Jones house; the tenancy became vacant soon after the Kiplings' return from Vermont, and Rudyard and Carrie and the children moved in just after John was born in 1897. In *Three Houses* Angela Thirkell (granddaughter of the Burne-Joneses) writes about sitting with Josephine in cousin Ruddy's study in The Elms as he read them some of the *Just So Stories*. Now the house is privately owned, and hidden behind the flint walls that Kipling found were not quite high enough to protect him from the day trippers from Brighton, who came over on buses hoping to catch a glimpse of the Laureate of Empire at work. But we were able to walk round the part of the gardens that are open to the public. The Kiplings came back to The Elms after Josephine had died in New York. 'The house and garden are full of the lost child,' reported Rudyard's father, 'and poor Rud told his mother how he saw her when a door opened, when a space was vacant at table – coming out of every green dark corner of the garden – radiant and – heartbreaking...'

The village church of St Margaret of Antioch (a martyr beheaded for her faith) sits on a hillock on the other side of the lane from The Elms, and has fabulous stained-glass windows – in glorious deep reds, blues and greens – designed by Burne-Jones and made by Morris & Co. Behind the altar soar three narrow windows of St Michael with Gabriel and Raphael on either side, each one with a small narrative window below: scarlet-winged St Michael slaying the dragon with a long green spear; Gabriel announcing to the Blessed Virgin Mary; Raphael leading a small child by the hand. On the north and south walls of the chancel, St Margaret with her foot on a red serpent, and opposite her the blue-robed BVM. Kipling's beloved Uncle Ned died in June 1898, and here, beneath these five windows, the box containing his ashes was placed on the drawing table from his studio, and the men of the family took it in turns to hold watch throughout the night. Kipling took the dawn watch. A commemorative plaque to Edward and Georgiana Burne-Jones is fixed into the outside wall of the church near the porch. The topography is not how I envisaged it from Kipling's description of Burne-Jones's ashes being lowered, by his son and daughter, into a moss-lined grave. A bit further down the slope stand the remains of a low-lying wooden structure, not unlike a small bed, which marks the grave of Angela Thirkell.

Squeezed into a corner of the Rudyard Kipling Museum, just down the lane, and on the first floor above the village library, is a mock-up of Kipling's study in The Elms, with a dusty and sinister life-size plaster cast of the man himself sitting at his desk.

Bateman's, near Burwash, deeper into Sussex: a beautiful sandstone Jacobean house with gables and tall chimneys, set at the end of a long avenue of trees, just as in Kipling's 'dead children' story "They", and surrounded by lawns, flower beds, and orchards of apple and pear. Very dark interior. Why did the Victorians and Edwardians go for all that olde worlde oak panelling? Perhaps it helped keep the rooms warmer in winter. I was surprised by the number of literary tourists: there were four or five people in each room. I couldn't find the photograph of Josephine that I am so keen to track down, and that for some reason I thought was here at Bateman's: she is in a white frock and sitting on a tiger-skin rug draped over an armchair. It was taken at Naulakha in

Vermont when she was three or four. Josephine was dead by the time Carrie and Rudyard bought Bateman's in 1902. However, the pastel portrait of her drawn by Lina Holbrook is propped up on one of the bedside tables: the picture is vague and fuzzy, really not very good at all. I think this was the picture that was brought over from Vermont by their driver/housekeeper the first Christmas after Josephine died: 1899, just before the family set sail for South Africa. I enquired after the photograph: one of the National Trust volunteers had never heard of it, and another said it was locked in the 'archive' on the top floor of the house and not available to the general public. I was disappointed.

18 September

Daniel Karlin's comments on my Kipling chapters arrived the day before I set off for Sussex, and since then I have had little time for the necessary digestion. His covering letter was hugely insightful, helpful, generous, and quite fiercely critical. Some of the issues he has raised I am aware of myself; some I knew but didn't know I knew; some I hadn't realized at all but as soon as I read what he said I saw he was absolutely right. What is the rationale behind telling the story in a back-and-forth way? If there is a rationale, he says, I need to state it. But if there ever was a rationale I have long forgotten it. Names: Rud or Ruddy or Rudyard or Kipling? Sometimes I use three different names on the same page. Why do I go on and on and on sneering at Cecil Rhodes for his high-pitched, squeaky voice ('as you keep mentioning,' notes Karlin)? My portrayal of Rhodes as nothing but a narcissistic racist makes anyone's warm feelings towards him (such as Rudyard's or Carrie's) a matter of delusion. I think Karlin has pinpointed a deep anxiety I harbour that someone might point a finger at me and because of my subject matter accuse me of being pro-imperialist or neocolonialist. That anxiety has fed into my neurotic repetitions about the evil incarnate that was Cecil Rhodes. I have drawn heavily on William Plomer's hostile biography, and Karlin remarks, 'I hold no brief for Rhodes but I hope you will be disconcerted if I tell you that I ended up disliking Plomer more than him.' Yes, I *am* disconcerted.

The following, however, is what is causing me the most pain: 'to be honest I think you need to do a bit more work on some of the critical accounts you give of the writings...', and he identifies my commentary on 'A Sahibs' War' as an example of my critical failings. I know he is absolutely right. But I am reeling from it. And feeling...scared. What if I prove incapable of attaining his high standards of scholarship and intelligent reading?

25 September

How right Karlin is: why do I tell it all to and fro, and back to front? I am embarking on a chronological rewrite of the first six early chapters – the ones that cover my subjects' early, pre-Boer War years – and I am also dealing slowly, carefully with Karlin's textual annotations.

29 September

And now, once again, I am away from home – no wonder it is taking me years to write this book – at the Padstow tai chi retreat. Last night I had a truly frightening nightmare: my son was taking me through the streets of a city full of murderers and lawlessness, and then I became separated from him and didn't know the address of where we were staying, or whereabouts it was.

I am feeling incredibly anxious about Kipling. What an idiot Daniel Karlin must think me. I know I should be positive, and use his comments to help me improve what I have written, and I *shall* do that, but at the moment, while I am not actually working on the book, all that is wrong with it expands to fill my mind. I feel crushed.

Lara Feigel told me she received some 'extremely difficult' criticism from Danny Karlin years back when he was supervising her MA on Proust at UCL. How did she respond? By falling madly in love with him! I laughed in amazement. I just couldn't imagine falling in love with anyone who criticizes my writing. Apparently back then Karlin was saturnine and handsome and constantly being fallen in love with. (Maybe he still is; I don't know.)

5 October

Thinking over what Lara told me, I am not so surprised. Don't we all long to be closely read? Yes, but not, in my case, criticized.

I have pulled apart and completely restructured the first two Kipling chapters. The story now starts with his birth. Oh my God. Why, oh why? Et cetera, and so on. *Of course* this is where it should start.

8 October

When Diana Hendry rang me on Saturday and asked how I was, she took me by surprise, and so I actually told her. I said that I was feeling crushed by Danny Karlin's comments: his pointing out my failure to fully engage with Kipling the writer, the clichés that litter my text, the infelicities of phrase. I also told her that I was suffering severe PMR pain; it is as bad as when I went down to 4 milligrams of prednisolone this time last year. Back then I went up to 7.5 milligrams and the pain eased up, but I don't want to go all the way up to 7.5 again.[7] On top of all else, I have chosen now as the time to grow out my hair dye and accept my natural colour, with the consequence that whenever I catch a glimpse of myself in the

---

7   Ha! Transcribing this journal a year later, after months of PMR agony and a huge increase in steroids, I am now trying desperately to get *down* to 7.5 milligrams: a dosage which seems like some marvellous dream of being almost on no drugs at all.

mirror (something I try to avoid), I see an unrecognizable white-haired woman staring back at me.

HB has reminded me that some people – Michael Dwyer and the anonymous Hurst reader – have read what I have already written and have liked it enough to want to publish it. Both she and Ismay say they really like my new-style white hair and that it does not make me look old; they are both wonderfully sympathetic listeners to my various complaints. I often think, What would I do without my daughters?

12 October

Diana listened carefully to my litany of woe. She emailed me later with a list of thoughtful questions about pain management, and questions about my book, and suggested I set aside my Kipling chapters for the moment.

15 October

The PMR pain is as bad as it has ever been. When I woke at 2am, it felt like the 4am or even the 6am pain, which is usually the most intensely painful in the whole twenty-four-hour cycle. I have difficulty climbing up and down the stairs.

23 October

'…a pretty woman in her mid-fifties with dark hair'. Oh, how I love Kent Haruf (introduced to me only last year by Diana). That description is from *Benediction*. A hundred lesser writers, women as well as men, would have written something like 'still a pretty woman' or 'pretty, although she was in her mid-fifties'.

26 October

Blood test results: CRP 32; ESR 37. No wonder I have been in agony. I went up to 7.5 milligrams of prednisolone, and as a week later that was having no effect at all, I continued upwards to 10 milligrams.

17 November

I have worked my way through Danny Karlin's notes in the margins of my typescript, and have written, 'Dealt with!' in big black felt tip on the covering sleeve of each chapter as I've finished it. What an alert reader he is. I have realized that many of his observations (or criticisms) – not just concerning the question of chronology – also hold true for my treatment of Mary Kingsley and Arthur Conan Doyle. I have already started to apply them.

Meanwhile I have more or less turned my 'Art of Rambling' lecture into an essay suitable for academic publication, mainly by adding footnotes and a long list of works cited, and shall send it to Julia in Silesia this week, after HB has read and OK'd it. And now, with the first two chapters each of Kipling and Kingsley sent off to Jenny and Michèle for our Group of Three meeting on Monday, I have found in my 'Art of Rambling' folder two pages from a version of the first Kingsley chapter I wrote two years ago that include a couple of paragraphs I long ago cut out but which strike me now, on rereading, as rather good. One of them is about the eccentric advice on West Africa that she received from friends before she set off (the dangers, disagreeables, diseases and so on); the other is about her friend Dennis Kemp, the Wesleyan missionary (the pragmatic Wesleyans being the only missionaries she had time for). Hmm. What shall I do? Reinstate them?

But now it is time, anyway, for me to grapple with the Arthur Conan Doyle chapters that I haven't looked at since December last year.

26 November

10 milligrams of prednisolone has alleviated the pain considerably.

I am now back at Tuesday-evening tai chi; I even managed the Friday-morning workshop, although my shoulders were on fire.

29 November

In the 'Books of the Year' edition of the *TLS*, Joyce Carol Oates has chosen *Uncertainties*, volumes 1, 2 and 3, edited by Brian J. Showers. She doesn't mention any individual stories (such as my own two). But even so! And she does mention the elegant appearance of the books.

8 December

Persistent drizzling rain at Thursday's RDA; the arena sploshy with mud. Only three children in the first session: Pip, the instructor, had them do a trotting race to finish, and Princess, with Alex on board, broke into a canter, to the leader's panic but to Alex's huge delight. All three children were grinning when they reached the rails.

12 December

Theresa May faces a vote of (no) confidence from the Tories tonight, after forty-eight (or more) of them sent in letters demanding one. Such a drama would be a source of innocent pleasure for us onlookers, were it not for the thought that these past two and a half years of power play among the Tories might still lead to us leaving Europe and becoming a rogue state – a banana monarchy. May's statement this morning was crammed full of her usual platitudes about being concerned only with the national interest. The Tory rebels waited until she was out of the country, struggling in Brussels, before sending in their letters, as if they were too scared to do it while she was actually, physically in this country.

18 December

Since Friday I have had a horrible tooth infection. It came on suddenly in the afternoon and quickly got worse. By Saturday it felt as if my mouth were crowded with teeth too tightly packed in and I couldn't close my jaw for the searing pain. It emanates from the top right, where I have had trouble before. I started taking co-codamol, so have been feeling befuddled on top of everything else. On Sunday I found an old tramadol in my desk drawer so I quickly swallowed that: even more befuddlement. Meanwhile I remembered that Doc Mason prescribed me some amoxycillin some years ago, 'just in case', before I went away somewhere – South Africa? Yes, I think it was when I went to Bloemfontein with Mon in 2015; he had just pulled out the crowned tooth that had caused me pain since 1978, and he prescribed the antibiotics in case the wound in the gum got infected. I found the dusty packet at the back of the top bathroom shelf, and started taking them on Sunday. Feeling very low indeed. I went to see Doc Mason yesterday afternoon. By then my lower jaw, throat and neck were throbbing. He ground off the tops of two or three of the teeth in my upper jaw so that I could close my mouth without a jabbing pain. I could not stop myself crying. As I was lying on the dental chair with my head below my feet, the tears were puddling in my ears.

I took two paracetamol this morning and by lunchtime the pain was noticeably diminished. Perhaps the antibiotics are kicking in at last, or the new antibiotics are more effective than the out-of-date ones. Christ, what must it have been like in the old days with no antibiotics?

22 December

Yesterday (Friday) our friends Cass and John came round for a solstice celebration. We hadn't seen them for some months, not since I started growing out my hair dye. 'Oh, your hair looks terrific!' they said, as soon as they came in. 'Have you coloured it, or is that natural?... Wonderful! It makes you look so youthful...', and so on. I love them!

Chapter 10

January – August 2019; London, Bristol, Home

3 January 2019

I am now, at last, on the delayed 9.47 to Paddington, after a fifty-minute wait on the windswept platform at Nailsea and Backwell. I am on my way to the British Library to read more of Mary Kingsley's letters to her publisher George Macmillan and a couple of her essays in the *National Review*, and to take another look at the second (1901) edition of *West African Studies*, which includes as an appendix the lecture she gave on 12 February 1900 at the Imperial Institute, during which she urged the British government to keep its promises in West Africa, and argued for the need to perceive the African as he really was, rather than 'dealing with him through a dream-thing, the fiend-child African of your imagination'. She had always been critical of Kipling's 'Half devil and half child'. She ended her lecture with 'Goodbye and fare ye well, for I am homeward bound.' It was the last lecture she ever gave. Three weeks later she set sail for Cape Town, and was dead within five months.

I can't believe it: those dumdum bullets have raised their (soft) noses once more. Talk about the return of the repressed! Yesterday I was working on chapter 8, the chapter that shows all three of them – Kingsley, Kipling and Conan Doyle – as they prepare for their departures and then take ship. As I was checking one or two of the page references in the first edition of Stephen Gwynn's *The*

Life of Mary Kingsley, my eye happened by chance to fall on the letter Kingsley wrote to John St Loe Strachey – her friend, and editor of *The Spectator* – from aboard the SS *Moor*. In my own text I had made a bit of a song and dance about her reporting to Strachey the rumour that she had heard on board ship about a large cache of dumdum bullets being held by the British in besieged Ladysmith, and how she told Strachey that the story was on no account for publication, as the use of dumdums was internationally banned. I wrote that in his biography Gwynn had honoured that injunction, even though thirty years had passed and the war was history. I thought he had honoured it because I first read the letter in the paperback edition of his *Life*, where it was heavily redacted without any indication that that was the case (no ellipses; no footnotes). When I later looked at the original letter from Kingsley in the Strachey archives and read this amazing story, I just assumed that Gwynn had carried out her wishes (as expressed to Strachey) for it to be hushed up. Oh, traitorous assumptions!

4 January

Sitting on the platform at Nailsea and Backwell for fifty minutes yesterday, waiting for the delayed train, chilled me to the bone. Still, the train was only twenty-five minutes late into Paddington. When I got to the British Library I had to go first to the reader registration room to renew my card as it runs out in three weeks' time. It took half an hour. Then, when I eventually got up to Manuscripts, the two volumes of Mary Kingsley's correspondence with George Macmillan were not there ready for me, because, the unsympathetic man behind the desk informed me, I had ordered them both *on the same ticket*, and that was not allowed. What? I had to blink away the tears that were welling up. Fortunately, the *National Review* volume for 1896 had been sent down from the reserve collection in Boston Spa, and the second edition of *West*

African Studies was waiting for me. A kind woman at the help desk helped me reorder the two volumes of correspondence – on two separate tickets.

I read 'The Development of Dodos', in which Kingsley attacks not just the missionaries' imposition on the people of West Africa of the doctrine of forgiveness of sin by repentance (which she believes shows utter ignorance of the traditional belief systems and laws of the local people), but also the missionaries' attempts to stop the liquor trade. This is one of her early articles on the subject. She compares Vauxhall Road on a Saturday night unfavourably with what she has seen in Old Calabar. Her belief that missionaries and colonial officials made their minds up first and ignored all evidence to the contrary would make her very unpopular in establishment circles. In the same volume of *National Review* I read 'The Throne of Thunder', a hilarious account of her stumbling ascent of Mount Cameroon in drenching rain and thick fog. By then the two volumes of Kingsley's correspondence with Macmillan had arrived: collated in the 1960s, bound in bright red, stamped with the name of the British Museum. The letters are more or less in date order, but they stop suddenly in August 1899. Why? Where are the rest of them? I had been hoping for some South Africa references, but no. All the early letters, dated 1896, are to do with the bits and pieces left by her father George Kingsley when he died in 1892 – the material that she would edit into *Notes on Sport and Travel*. I hadn't realized how closely involved Mary and her brother Charley were over this. What a tiresome fellow Charley sounds! He told Macmillan, untruthfully, that he had burned all his father's notes.

The Manuscripts room closes at 5pm, so I had to arrange for everything to be transferred one floor down, to Rare Books.

The BL is crammed full of students taking up every seat and table outside the reading rooms, and in the overpriced, underlit café, chattering like flocks of starlings. Where do they all come from? I guess from London universities that just don't have the library capacity for all of them. Perhaps the BL acts as an overflow library space. I find it dark, gloomy, oppressive to the spirits. In Manuscripts there aren't even any desk lights. I came out feeling... extinguished.

11 January

I suddenly remembered that my friend the writer and photographer Sue Swingler, who has been suffering from PMR for not quite as long as I have, sent me an email before Christmas with some internet-gleaned advice on a way to effectively reduce prednisolone dosage. It is a tip for when you have got down to a low dosage but are finding it hard to reduce further: take half a milligram less for one day, then return to the previous dosage for five days, then half a milligram less for one day, then back up for four days, and so on. I think it's worth a try to get down from 9 milligrams to 8, as in fact I went back up to 9 ten days ago because being on 8 was too painful. Onwards...

15 January

I went to Bristol's Central Reference Library yesterday to read Mary Kingsley's April 1898 article about the liquor trade in West Africa in *The Fortnightly Review* – for the second time. I discovered that in my own text I had written the title of the article – 'Liquor Traffic with West Africa' – inaccurately: 'in' rather than 'with', and inserting 'The'. I was shocked at my own carelessness. In the article Kingsley censures *The Times* for its anti-liquor-trade stance and for its belief in the superiority of the English race over all others, and she questions the existence of the evidence on which it bases its judgements. She is Swiftian in her satire: controlled, ruthless, and even scatological. I am not sure I fully appreciated her panache on my first reading.

I love the Central Reference Library: the way daylight pours through the glass roof, the generous bay windows with their thick-topped polished tables, the elegant stacks. There are never too many people; often only a few old men snoozing in the wooden armchairs. It could not be more different from the dark, crowded, noisy cavern of the British Library.

I read Anna Burns's *Milkman* (a Booker prize-winner) just before Christmas, and last week Olga Tokarczuk's *Drive Your Plow Over the Bones of the Dead* (the latter a Christmas present from Jill Nicholls; Julia Szołtysek earlier sent me *Flights* as a gift: Julia used to give English-conversation lessons to Tokarczuk). What excellent novels – both of them comic, dark, engaged with patriarchal power, and both of them narrated by wise women.

18 January

I'm on the train at Temple Meads on my way to London for the launch of my brother Mark's new book about representations of Christianity in European films of the Golden Age, *Believing in Film*. He is holding it at the Savile Club, which opened its doors to the twenty-four-year-old Rudyard Kipling when he burst upon the London literary scene in 1890 with 'The Ballad of East and West'.

On Wednesday I finished chapter 10: Conan Doyle doctoring in Bloemfontein at the Café Enterique, Boulevard des Microbes. Yesterday I finished the chapter again. And then I finally, *finally* finished it this morning.

1 February

On Wednesday, as the dog and I approached the dry pond beneath the oak in the corner of Littlewood Field, a hare started up from the oak litter just under my feet. She bounded away – pale brown body, black tips to her ears – and was gone through the hedge and vanished in a couple of seconds. She was so swift the dog didn't even glimpse her. I suggested to Michèle and Jenny that she was a sign of blessing for us all. God knows I need a blessing.

I am exhausted by the countless decisions I have to make as I rewrite my chapters. Sometimes I wish someone else could make the decisions, or at least some of them, anyway.

It snowed last night. My hands are blocks of ice.

2 February

Imbolc/St Brigid's Day; also Candlemas. Halfway between the winter solstice and the spring equinox. The goddess Brigid was celebrated, thanked, perhaps appeased on Imbolc. Clever old Christians slipping in their St Brigid, and their own festival of fire and light that they call Candlemas. Later I shall light candles. I remember teaching with Michèle at Tŷ Newydd, maybe twenty years ago, and one of our students – a brown-haired, hazel-eyed poet – took us out one clear, moonlit night to an ancient, sacred well – a St Brigid's Well. He led the way – very fast, so we had to run to keep up – through a dark forest, and into a clearing with a small, low-walled well in its centre; we looked down and saw the moon shining in its depths. As Michèle and I climbed out of his car on our return to Tŷ Newydd, he caught our hands, one of us after the other, kissed them, and saluted us as goddesses. I felt overwhelmed by the honour – a double honour because I was sharing it with Michèle – and by how powerful he made me feel. As if, however briefly, I really were a goddess.

I have increased my prednisolone dose to 10 milligrams to see if I can get any improvement from 8, but so far there is little difference. I have a constant pain in my chest and shoulders, especially in the left shoulder, and this morning I thought my left hip was going to give way. I could put hardly any weight at all on my left leg. I am dragged down into dreariness. My goddess self seems very distant.

20 February

Down to 9 milligrams of prednisolone, and pretty bloody painful.

I had agreed with my editor, Farhaana Arefin, that this week I would send her the finished manuscript of my book, but when at the end of last week I looked properly at the Hurst submission guidelines (rather than, as previously, just running my eye over them), I saw I had to submit the manuscript with all its notes and references, acknowledgements, bibliography, and so on, and so on. I felt utterly disheartened. I have rewritten and rewritten and rewritten; now I just want the bloody thing off my hands. There are times when I *hate* it, when I'm bored by it, when I can't bear to think that maybe I've cut out something that should be in, or that I've made some fearful mistake. I just want it to go – and of course I am desperate for someone to read the whole thing, and to say, 'Yes, this is good.'

I wrote a panicky email to Farhaana saying, help, I can't do this. Later in the afternoon, when I had calmed down, I wrote again and apologized. She emailed back, very reassuring: we've got plenty of time, don't worry etc. Today I started on the references and bibliography; although it is desperately slow it is not impossible. I have already emailed someone from the Conan Doyle Estate about permissions. And actually, even though I have to change the paragraph layout throughout (double line space, no indent), at least I can insert my own footnotes and present them as a fait accompli. That is the upside of Hurst's hands-off attitude. Sometimes when I hear other writers talk of their many meetings with their editors, their lengthy conversations, their joint wrestling with this or that textual problem, I become envious. I yearn for an editor with whom I could wrestle, argue, even just talk things over. But on good days I am content with my own decisions and pleased that I am free to make them.

Writing the footnotes has given me a great deal of pleasure. On reflection I know that it is better to do all this now – the notes, references and so on – rather than have to go back to them later. If I have to spend time now looking up references in libraries, well, I shall just have to do that.

21 February
Both Michèle and Jenny think my three final chapters, on the 'afterlives' of my three subjects, are ready to go. They have suggested a number of changes/improvements at sentence and paragraph level – they are both very good at that close line-editing – which I haven't yet looked at, but basically they think the chapters are OK. What an unutterable relief.

26 February
Weirdly and suddenly, yesterday morning as C and I were returning from dropping the Nissan off at the garage for its MOT, I had a crippling attack of heartburn. Waves of pain washed through me. As soon as we got back I had to go and lie down. Again in the early afternoon I felt odd and weak, and went and lay down again. I keep on thinking of the various people I have known (such as Alastair from up the road) who said, 'Oh, I feel a bit funny – I'll just go and have a bit of a lie down.' And then they were found dead on the bed an hour later.

I am creeping on through my notes and references.

20 March
I sent off my manuscript this morning, my son having amalgamated the three separate sections of it for me without losing any of the formatting. Genius! It has taken me one month to do all the notes and references and fiddly bits. 595 endnotes. Blimey. I hope that's not too off-putting. Perhaps I could ask Hurst to set them in a tiny

point size so they don't take up too many pages. But still, it's done – done! I can barely remember now what the actual *text* is like. Also, I am pleased that in a book that might be thought of as quite masculine in subject matter – I mean that it is about war, and two of its three subjects are not just any old men, but famous Manly, possibly even Great Men – I have cunningly managed to bookend the endnotes with references to women writers (Olive Schreiner number 1, Rose Macaulay number 595).

As I was coming home from tai chi last night I suddenly thought, Oh my God, what if the house goes up in flames tonight? (Memories of the occasion when I was driving home in the dark with HB and the lane was suddenly thick with fog – only it wasn't fog, but smoke, and as we turned into the drive we saw flames coming out of the chimney. And once the firemen had arrived and poured water down the chimney it ran along all the old internal beams and came out in thick dark streaks down the walls, and it was as if we had been transported into *The Shining*.) So, as soon as I came through the door I rushed to my laptop and emailed a copy of the whole book to HB, just in case, and then heaved a sigh of relief. What if 500 pages had gone up in smoke? And my laptop?

The house did not burn down last night, and this morning I whizzed the text off to Farhaana with an anxious note asking her to tell me that it had arrived safely with all the formatting intact…and received an out-of-office reply saying she's not back until tomorrow.

Yesterday in the Arts and Social Sciences Library's new Special Collections room – they have been promoted from the basement up to the first floor – I asked Ian the archivist if I could photograph W. T. Stead's anti-war pamphlet *The War in South Africa*. 'Do you know when he died?' he asked.

'Yes, indeed: he went down on the *Titanic*.'

Ian looked taken aback. Then I realized he had been asking so as to find out whether the pamphlet was out of copyright, and had not expected to receive a detailed reply. It was the first opportunity I have had to tell someone that poor old Stead – editor of *The Pall Mall Gazette* and *The Review of Reviews*, one-time spiritualist, and friend of Arthur Conan Doyle before his anti-war campaigns drove Doyle into a fury – drowned when the *Titanic* went down. I felt obscurely pleased.

26 March

For the first time in what feels like forever I don't have to rewrite a chapter, nor plough through citations… I'm going to go through the notes that I made on the Dec/Jan/Feb rewrite, and see which of them are outstanding, but that seems like quite a pleasurable task. This relaxed mood depends, of course, on the assumption that Farhaana is not going to email me and demand huge changes or cuts…

Meanwhile, C and I took the train to London yesterday to see the Dorothea Tanning exhibition at Tate Modern. Amazing! Huge canvases, wonderful soft sculptures – a whole sitting room with weird soft shapes coming out of the wall, breaking through the wallpaper. As Tanning herself described it: 'sinister and also banal'. And the Pierre Bonnard exhibition on a different floor: Bonnard painted his wife Marthe nude throughout their lives together (forty plus years), and she never grew old in his paintings: always the same young, smooth limbs and high breasts. I'm not sure quite what I think about that. I think maybe it is a bit creepy. Even, perhaps, sinister and also banal?

28 March

White waves of blackthorn blossom are racing across the bare hedges; the oaks are fuzzed with leaf.

11 April

From the 'NB' column in last week's *TLS*:

> Q: Why can't you starve in the desert?
> A: Because you can eat the sand which is there.
> Q: Who brought the sandwiches there?
> A: Noah sent Ham, and his descendants mustered and bred.

One of the reasons I am fond of Conan Doyle is his penchant for riddles, such as:

> Q: Why did the owl 'owl?
> A: Because the woodpecker would peck 'er.

I bet he would have enjoyed the sandwiches riddle.

14 May

As I was walking down Piccadilly last Wednesday, on my way to my first ever meeting with the Kipling Society, at the annual luncheon at the Army & Navy Club, I felt something suddenly give at the back of my right knee. It felt like a small, sharp click – not exactly painful, but odd, somehow not right. I was aware of it throughout lunch, during which I was seated next to a good-looking photographer and her partner (I would guess 'lover', or even 'married lover': I detected something illicit in the air). The partner had spent three weeks in the Polana Hotel in Maputo at some point in the 1990s when he was working with BP and negotiating coal-mining contracts with the Mozambican government. Maputo was Lourenço Marques back when Mozambique was a colony of the Portuguese. The Polana is where British secret agent Maurice Castle waits to be reunited with his black South African girlfriend Sarah in Graham Greene's *The Human Factor*, after she has escaped into Mozambique from out of the clutches of the dreaded South African security services. And very possibly where Roger Casement stayed in 1900 when he was spying on the transport of arms through to the Boer Republics. I wonder when it was built – I guess around the same time as the Mount Nelson Hotel in Cape Town. (No: I later found out it was built in 1922, six years after Casement was executed by the British government.)

Professor Daniel Karlin gave a brainy post-lunch lecture on Kipling and Robert Browning, and in particular Browning's 'Fra Lippo Lippi', which Kipling drew on in his memoir to illuminate his miserable childhood years in the 'House of Desolation'. It was the first time I had set eyes on Karlin; I could easily see how, twenty years ago, Lara might have fallen for him and his 'difficult criticism'. At the end of his talk I intruded myself into the group who were hosting him as guest speaker, awkwardly introduced myself, and quickly retreated. Nice Mike Kipling, who is secretary of the Society, said to make sure to keep them informed about my book, and perhaps, when it comes out, I would like to address the Society.

Train home from Paddington; drive home from the station. By then my knee was really hurting. The next morning the whole leg, from knee to ankle, was badly swollen. C said I should see a GP as soon as possible. Only very rarely does C, a doctor himself, suggest I seek medical advice. It always makes me nervous when he does. The doctor looked at my leg, and picked up the phone on his desk to ring Weston General. He told me to get in the car and drive straight there for a Doppler scan. By then I was really scared. However, the scan showed that it is not a thrombosis, which of course, I now realize, is what both C and the GP thought it might be. Instead it is a ruptured Baker's cyst which is leaking fluid down the veins of my calf, making it swell and harden. It is extremely painful. Presumably it has been brought on by the PMR, and perhaps too by the lowered immunity caused by long-term steroids. Oh God. I'm creeping around like my ninety-seven-year-old mother-in-law.

This morning as I was staggering along with the dog I found one of our elderly neighbours completely stationary at the side of the lane, leaning almost horizontally across his wheelie walker. As I was escorting him home, very slowly indeed, a man stopped his car and asked if we needed help. I hope it was my elderly neighbour whom he thought needed it, but perhaps it was me.

17 May
Premier Inn, Earl's Court. I just love Premier Inns. They are so restfully predictable. Last night at the French Institute, Mo Sutton's film *Daughters of de Beauvoir* was extremely good: in it nine or ten women talk fascinatingly about feminism and de Beauvoir. It is as fresh as if it were made yesterday rather than thirty years ago. The discussion panel consisted of Mo, me, Margaret Drabble, Mithu Sanyal (who has just published a book on rape with Verso), and the moderator Kate Muir. The film didn't start until eight, the panel until after nine. I was exhausted and slightly panicked. I mean, Mo had invited me because I was editor of the book (of the film) at The Women's Press all those years ago, but I'm no expert on de B., and in fact there were many people in the audience who knew her work better than I did. I fear I said all sorts of random things. There was a large audience: about 150, women and men, lots of French people. I got the impression that everything the Institute puts on is well attended. The event was held in their lovely, comfortable, state-of-the-art cinema. They didn't offer any of us a fee, and only grudgingly paid my – very cheap – train fare. Elisa Segrave was there with some friends, one of whom had worked at Quartet in the 1980s and said how much she had admired us women at The

Women's Press. My brothers and I have known Elisa since we were teenagers and living in Edinburgh. She was a friend of their friend Andrew Davenport, who died very young in a mysterious water-skiing accident in Hong Kong where he was working as a financial journalist. My mother was very fond of Elisa; so are we. She wrote one of the first cancer memoirs, *Diary of a Breast*, which I remember (it is a long time since I read it) as darkly humorous. She told me a droll story about marching in Jean-Paul Sartre's funeral procession in Paris in 1980 (where she bumped into my friend Jill Nicholls), which I urged her to write up and submit to JC at the *TLS* for the 'Freelance' column. I'm always urging friends to do that: I think that after my two rejections I want to see if any woman (apart from A. E. Stallings, but maybe it's the initials that does the trick there) can ever actually please him.

I would have liked to chat for longer, but I was on my last legs – or, rather, last leg. My right calf is very swollen, hard and painful, as is the knee itself.

23 May

C and I went to London again on Tuesday for Michèle's birthday gathering in a narrow old house with wooden stairs, in a street off Queen Square. The party was gloriously eccentric and involved a Debussy recital, a young woman from the Guildhall singing a poem by Verlaine, all sorts of stuff about Balzac – Balzac? Apparently it was his birthdate too – and then drinks and canapés. The singer became quite tipsy and shouted a lot. Nell Dunn, whose grandfather fought in the Boer War, told me a story about an encounter she had on the number 14 bus a couple of weeks ago:

Man on bus: You look like Nell Dunn.
Nell: I am Nell Dunn.
Man: Oh, and are you still writing?

Nell: Yes. In fact I've just finished a book and I'm looking for a publisher.

Man: I am a publisher.

And indeed he was an editor at Hodder & Stoughton. Ha ha ha! My fingers are crossed for her.

Nell's grandfather – the Earl of Rosslyn – was captured twice by the Boers, and wrote a memoir which he called *Twice Captured*. He was one of what seems like a largish number of memoir-writing English aristos rattling around in South Africa. I have included one of the other ones in my chapter 7, who wrote under the name of Trooper 8008 and who is sharp and funny about the useless training given to him and his fellow volunteers in the Imperial Yeomanry before they set off for South Africa at the beginning of 1900. I must try and get hold of Nell's grandfather's memoir. Nell told me that when her grandmother went to register his death, the registrar's clerk asked her what job her husband had had. She replied, 'Peer of the realm'; the clerk wrote down, 'Unemployed'.

There was a lot of standing up at Michèle's party and the next day I could barely walk. It was a trial to get back home. However, yesterday I kept my leg up for most of the day, and this morning it is not quite so bad, although still extremely painful. It will take two or three months, said Dr Davies (on whom I have rather a crush), for the fluid to be absorbed, and even then the calf may remain larger than it used to be. As they said that my PMR would be done and dusted within the year, and here I am, still suffering three years on, I can't say I am sanguine about Dr Davies's three-month prognosis.

4 June

The final read-through of my manuscript. I lie on my back on the sofa with my monstrous leg propped up on a tower of cushions and read the pages out loud, marking with a pencil where I might need to make a change; later on I sit up with my leg protected by a low IKEA table that the girls went out and bought for me, and make the changes that I've marked. One chapter a day is as much as I can manage. Today I remembered a reference to Conan Doyle wanting to send copies of his *The War in South Africa* to the exiled Boers on St Helena so that they could learn from its pages the truth about the conflict in which they had so foolishly engaged. When I couldn't locate the reference I dug out my 'outcuts' folder. Big mistake! I started to flick through page after page of paragraphs that once were in my text but that at one stage or another I decided to cut. I was thinking, Oh, that one's interesting…and that one… This way madness lies. I have now closed the folder and put it away.

Today is the anniversary of Mary Kingsley's dramatic ocean burial off Cape Point, when her coffin refused to sink and danced away with her over the glittering waves.

7 June

Yesterday I sent off my finished manuscript to Hurst (again!), I sincerely hope for the last time. I think that it's done, finished… I've answered almost all the questions that I asked myself in the last two final readings of the whole text. As for the few – the very few – that I have failed to answer: *tant pis.*

I have asked Michael and Farhaana to allow me to meet up with them to discuss the title, cover, illustrations, map, and index. Both of them appear, however, to have gone to ground.

11 June

Now that I've sent off my manuscript, tomorrow I'm chairing an event with Tracy K. Smith (Poet Laureate of the USA and author of a wonderful memoir, *Ordinary Light*), and then I have no more public events until Bart van Es in Wells in October.

Michael Dwyer is 'very happy' with *Something of Themselves* as a main title. The right decision, I believe. The subtitle: *Kipling, Kingsley, Conan Doyle and the Anglo-Boer War.*

13 June

Both knees are getting more painful day by day. In the left one it must be the PMR; in the right one, PMR plus the damage caused by the ruptured Baker's cyst. They are both swollen and hard to bend; the right (damaged) one is much worse than the left. I am wearing compression bandages.

Swallows are swooping over the next-door field, zipping past my legs, gleaming indigo, then showing a flash of white underbelly as they bank and turn. This morning I stopped for a moment to admire a gloriously iridescent turquoise dragonfly that was hovering close to my (bandaged) knee, when suddenly – whoosh – a swallow darted by. Goodbye, dragonfly.

24 June

I have at last – I think – worked my way through the tangle of Kipling copyright and come out on the other side. It has taken me since March: moving from the National Trust to United Agents (circling round and round there for a long time; no one wanted to take on the responsibility) to The Keep at Sussex, with the Kipling Society (Mike Kipling has been very helpful: he thinks *nothing* is in copyright) and Thomas Pinney (editor of *The Letters of Rudyard Kipling*) on the way. The only material that is not in the public domain (as far as I can see) is the unpublished stuff. It has been a marathon. I was massively anxious when I started out, but now... well, I think it's all OK. Picture permissions are another anxiety, but for the moment I shall park that on one side.

29 June

Although the swelling in my right calf has gone down, the PMR seems to have taken up residence in both knees. Every morning I am in crippling pain. The blonde-ponytailed rheumatology consultant whom I was allowed to see last week at the Bristol Royal Infirmary could have hardly cared less. She told me to stick to 7.5 milligrams of prednisolone. But it simply doesn't work. She wasn't listening to me but I felt weirdly unable to challenge her. She said I had lost muscle tone in my legs and was suffering from 'lack of condition'. She prescribed 'gentle exercise', and insisted it was now merely a question of 'rehabilitation'.

I asked her, 'Are you going to do a blood test?'

'Oh no, I don't think we need to do a blood test.'

At the end of the consult she said she wouldn't need to see me again. I felt dismissed as a malingerer and moaner.

1 July

The pain in my knees is almost unendurable. Today I couldn't finish my normal walk, but got only as far as the meeting house before turning back, in tears. Of course it must be the PMR: I can feel that familiar fiery pain in both knees. I'm going to have to make a huge effort, grit my teeth, and make the changes to my manuscript that I need to make before the copy-editor gets started on it. I don't think that it's a great deal of work, but I feel as if I am digging into my very last ounce of energy. Really what I want to do is lie on my bed and cry. If the GP who is ringing me this afternoon – one I haven't spoken to before – doesn't come up with a suggestion for strong painkillers that actually work, then I'm going to have to increase the prednisolone tomorrow. But by how much? Should I double it to 15 milligrams? What a hideously backward step that seems. James has suggested that alongside the prednisolone I try a non-steroidal anti-inflammatory such as Celebrex.

Each day is a struggle to get through to 5 or 6pm, when the pain begins to ease off slightly. And then I can have a drink, which certainly helps. I am happy to be in bed by ten because I am so exhausted by the daily struggle, but I know that I'll be waking up to excruciating pain at 5am.

Thank God this didn't happen while I was actually writing the book. Things began to go wrong soon after I had submitted it: first the pain in the knees, and then the ruptured Baker's cyst which I think has exacerbated everything.

2 July

I have got a prescription for Celebrex, despite a fair amount of teeth-sucking at the end of the telephone – I spoke to the duty doctor, not my dear Dr Davies – and only as a one-off. What is it with these doctors and their reluctance to prescribe painkillers that are actually effective?

6 July

On Thursday I went into the Hurst offices in Great Russell Street for a meeting with Michael and Farhaana. This was the first time I had met Farhaana. My brother Julian escorted me so as to help me negotiate the tube, and to carry my suitcase up the Hurst stairs. We were going to discuss illustrations – Michael generously says I can have sixteen pages of them – and cover design. Both Michael and Farhaana praised my book hugely: 'beautifully written', 'full of surprises' and so on. I was so *pleased*. And OUP want to publish it in the USA. I had put a load of photos of potential illustrations onto a stick, which Farhaana downloaded onto Michael's desktop. The first photo he clicked on was – OMG, how embarrassing – a group photo of my daughter's wedding. I blushed. When it was time for me to leave, Farhaana kindly called an Uber and Michael put me into it to take me all the way south to Walworth for a Group of Three meeting at Michèle's.

Later, on the train home, I glanced at my phone (always a mistake) and saw an email from someone at United Agents (representatives of the National Trust, to whom Kipling left his estate), demanding £650 for permission to quote Kipling and any material held in The Keep. What? At once the lovely feeling I'd had all day – that my book had been read and appreciated and that everything was going to be OK – was swept away by a wave of anxiety.

16 July

An email from Routledge requesting permission to reprint a chapter from *In the Chinks*, in some short-print-run, high-priced (library?) anthology. I said yes, but could they please see their way to paying me a small fee as I don't have a salaried academic job – say, £200 or £300? Almost by return: yes, £300, and they even attached a template invoice for the fee. Now I wish I'd asked for £500. Even so, jolly nice, and it just shows: when you make demands, you (sometimes) get results.

19 July

This morning I sent my final, final (I think I have said this before, probably more than once) manuscript to Farhaana. I later got an email from United Agents, to whom I had written querying whether the National Trust actually had any rights at all in the unpublished Kipling material, and what on earth made them think they had rights in a telegram from Cecil Rhodes? Their email in reply said that the request for £650 for permissions was all a big mistake, and I can quote for free. Very satisfactory. But what if I hadn't challenged the original demand?

24 July

Yet another unelected Prime Minister has been foisted upon us: the liar, fornicator and blusterer Boris Johnson. As leader of the Conservative Party he is de facto Prime Minister – which means that a tiny proportion of the population, all of them Tories, has inflicted their choice on the whole country. There is surely something absurd in this. Just as there was something absurd in declaring war to win the franchise for our compatriots (or greedy adventurers) in a country far away, when the vast majority of the inhabitants of that country were denied voting rights on grounds of colour, and the majority of those who went to fight in the name of Britain and her empire were themselves disenfranchised at home.

Conan Doyle, to give him his due, really did believe that the Uitlanders were being treated unfairly. I suspect Kipling really didn't care about them. He was interested in the game being pursued by his politician friends: Rhodes, Milner, Chamberlain. Johnson has chosen Brexit as his game, and everyone will have to live with the consequences.

8 August

About three weeks ago I had a telephone consultation with Dr Singh at the surgery and asked him to please authorize a blood test so that I could go to my appointment with Dr Davies (booked three weeks in advance) with the results. The debilitating – nay, crippling – pain that I've been suffering since May must be a PMR flare-up; either that or it's something else that needs dealing with, now. I know perfectly well that it is not the result of 'weak muscles' or 'lack of condition', as the ponytailed rheumatologist at the BRI wished me to believe.

The results of my blood test: ESR 60 (normal is between 5 and 10); CRP 47 (normal is 3 or 4). These are higher markers of inflammation than I believe I have ever had, higher even than when I was first diagnosed three years ago, before I had ingested a single corticosteroid.

The thing is, I *knew*. After three years of it I am pretty familiar with how my body feels at various levels of inflammation. I have become expert at fine distinctions between different levels of pain. I recognize the difference between 2am pain and 6am pain. But in some weird way I had believed Dr Ponytail when she said everything was fine and it was just a matter of rehabilitation. I am usually pretty confident when it comes to dealing with professional people – and why wouldn't I be, considering I share their education, privileges, social capital and so on? – but somehow I didn't dare contradict her. She should have ordered a blood test. Why on earth didn't she? Since then I have suffered nearly two months of excruciating, debilitating, unnecessary pain.

Anyway, and at last, nice Dr Davies advised me to go up from 7.5 to 10 milligrams: the increase should kick in within a couple of days, he said, and if not, get back to him, and meanwhile book another blood test for a fortnight's time. Well, it's day four now, and the extra 2.5 milligrams has made no discernible difference, so I'm going to go right up to 15 milligrams, and I shall let Dr Davies know in due course, i.e. after the fact.

Have I ever been completely pain-free on doses of 8 or 9 or 10 milligrams? I have a horrid suspicion the answer is no.

10 August

Yesterday I increased my prednisolone dose to 15 milligrams. This morning, for the first time in three months, I walked up and down the stairs like I used to (albeit a bit more slowly), rather than sideways, one step at a time, while clutching the banister.

Chapter 11

August – December 2019; Home, London

23 August 2019

For my birthday C gave me Adam (of *Countryfile*) Henson's book about rare breeds; in the chapter on old breeds of cow, Henson tells us that the last ever Alderney cow was shot and eaten by the Nazis when they occupied Alderney. It was smaller and gentler than the Jersey, more 'gazelle-like,' says Adam. He references 'The King's Breakfast', and also *Cranford*'s Miss Betsy Barker who loves her Alderney like a daughter. It reminded me that it has been ages since I've read *Cranford*... Oh, what joy! Miss Barker's cow falls into a lime pit and loses all its hair. Captain Brown advises her that she'll have to clothe it in a flannel waistcoat and flannel drawers if she wants it to survive; if it were him, however, he'd just shoot it. Miss Barker of course makes it a waistcoat and drawers of grey flannel, to the delight of the Cranfordians, who turn out en masse to watch it walk out to pasture, fully clothed. As our narrator, young Mary Smith, says, you don't get sights like that in London!

Then I thought I would reread *Mary Barton*, Mrs Gaskell's first novel, written soon after the death of her young son from scarlet fever, and on the back of which Charles Dickens offered to publish her in *Household Words*...and so we got *Cranford*. So *many* dead children in *Mary Barton*. Yes, some of it is (as people say) quite sentimental, but it is powerful, gripping stuff nonetheless, especially the scenes with the factory hands and their desperate measures (such as throwing vitriol in the face of a strike-breaker – imagine what the *Daily Mail* would make of that), and the edge-of-the-seat boat chase at the end. This made me think that, as I am writing a talk for an RLF podcast about the naming of biographical subjects (I mean how a biographer refers to them), I would read Mrs Gaskell's biography of Charlotte Brontë and see how she deals with the problem. I have never read it before. I had heard – from where? I don't know – that Mrs G. skirted round the issue of Branwell Brontë's drunkenness, and generally left out all the bad bits about life in Haworth Parsonage. To my surprise I have found that she paints a grim enough picture of a cold, neglectful father (a clergyman like Kipling's grandfather George Macdonald) who fucked his wife to death, carelessly allowed his two eldest daughters to die, spoiled and indulged his only son and encouraged him to drink, and didn't give a toss about Charlotte, Emily and Anne as long as they kept quiet and out of his way, and preferably out of the house, earning their own livings. Naturally, clever Mrs Gaskell doesn't actually *say* all of the above; the reader is invited to infer it.

30 August

Two days ago, on Wednesday, Boris Johnson sent a trio of knaves up to Balmoral to get the Queen to sign off on his 'prorogation' of Parliament: the closure of Parliament for five weeks so that he, Johnson, our unelected Prime Minister, can push through a no-deal Brexit. They call this 'taking back control'.

7 September

Since the above, our power-greedy PM has withdrawn the whip from twenty-one of his MPs (i.e. thrown them out of the Tory Party), including various former Ministers, former Chancellors and so on; has insisted on a general election and had that voted down (so far – why are they always voting on things over and over again?) by a coalition of MPs; has said that he would rather 'die in a ditch' than let the UK stay in the EU beyond 31 October; and has shamelessly used a phalanx of police officers in West Yorkshire as a backdrop to an election speech. Yesterday Amber Rudd resigned from the cabinet, saying Johnson was not actually engaging in any negotiations with the EU in Brussels. The opposition have voted that he can't call an election unless 'no deal' is removed as an option, and there are three court cases ongoing against his illegal prorogation. Yet the BBC continues to find a seemingly never-ending supply of knaves and fools to wheel out in support of this loathsome man.

Meanwhile on Wednesday I went to London for Hurst's fiftieth anniversary party, to which I took Michèle. Tall Jon Snow hosted a quiz on global affairs; there were loads of young people laughing, talking, and having a good time; lashings of nice wine, and mountains of delicious food: samosas, pakoras, bhajis, then bowls of biriyani and raita. Michèle and I spoke to Michael Dwyer's wife Rachel, who is a professor of Indian (languages?) at SOAS University of London and who seems a very good egg. I introduced myself to Susan Williams, author of the excellent *Who Killed Hammarskjöld?: The UN, the Cold War and White Supremacy in Africa.* She was the initial reader for *S is for Samora,* and recommended that Michael publish it. Another good egg – obviously. Earlier Michèle and I had a cup of tea in a café in Russell Square Gardens and then visited an exhibition of photographs by Gerty Simon in the Wiener Holocaust Library on the Square (I had spotted a poster for it in the lift coming up from the bowels of the earth at Russell Square tube station). There was a photo of Judith Kerr as a young girl, and a number of fine self-portraits. I didn't get home until after midnight.

On Friday I sent off my Writers Aloud essay, on how biographers name their subjects, to Steve Cook at the RLF. It is partly about my own unconscious gender biases, which I saw in the way I often call Mary Kingsley 'Mary' while referring to my two men, Kipling and Doyle, by their surnames. He responded that it was 'great' (thank you, Steve!) and that I should proceed with recording it for the podcast. Meanwhile I've been reading Sara Ahmed's utterly brilliant *Living a Feminist Life* and there's a bit in it about how she was introduced to a gathering of students by her first name when all the other professors (exclusively white and male) were introduced as Professor So-and-So. I have quoted her in my essay.

8 October

I have returned from our trip to Athens to visit A to the nightmare of gathering illustrations for my book, which I had fondly imagined (oh, what an idiot I am) I would do together with some clever person from Hurst; I thought that we would discuss together, make choices, and then she would cleverly find the best image. Oh no, oh no. I am doing all of it: choosing, sourcing, finding, clearing permission. It wouldn't be so bad if I had realized back in July that I would be solely in charge of this. Why didn't I realize it? Now I discover that it all has to be in by – I think – next week. And how can I tell whether an image I find is 'high-res' or not? And the Kipling permissions are a 'Pandora's box', to use the phrase used by the man from Bateman's earlier this year, or indeed a can of worms.

HB and J came out at the weekend and were very helpful at finding images for me on the internet, and I ran through all my 'possibles' with HB and together we made a selection. It is so incredibly helpful to talk things through with someone. That is what I had imagined I would be doing with someone at Hurst.

18 October

I am still struggling with getting all the illustrations for the book. I had utterly *no idea* how much work this would entail.

27 October

Within the last ten days: RLF interview/essay recording + chairing a panel on George Orwell for the Festival of Ideas + in conversation with Bart van Es at Wells Literary Festival. I am exhausted. Another three days to go on my proofs. Eight chapters left, plus all the end bits. But the illustrations went off to the typesetter on Friday. Now that was a real piece of work.

2 November

I sent off the proof corrections on Tuesday night: 29 October, thereby just meeting the deadline. Then on Wednesday and Thursday I had a bit of toing and froing, including the illustrations and the list of illustrations, and then yesterday evening Farhaana sent me a few final queries from *her* set of proofs. So, I think that's *nearly* it. Second proofs sometime next week…

12 November

I corrected second proofs on Saturday: as always, mistakes had crept in where changes had been made in the first proofs. Doubtless new mistakes will creep in around these new corrections. I rewrote a sentence that was rewritten during the edit, in the section on Arthur Conan Doyle in Egypt, about al-Mahdi and the Khalifa, but then in the proofread it was rewritten all over again. I have told myself not to be precious about it.

14 November

Sleety snow this morning. It rained all night, the ground was sodden anyway, and RDA has been cancelled. But thank God it's not (yet) like it is in Yorkshire, with villages evacuated all along the River Don (and apparently there is looting of abandoned houses – but looting by whom?), and Venice is now underwater. Meanwhile down south in Australia bush fires are raging.

In this ghastly election campaign the Tory press are going for the 'Corbyn is a friend of terrorists' line, which, guess what, is picked up by the BBC, who are eager to show footage of people shouting 'terrorist' at him, making out that there are thousands of them, when in reality there is only a handful.

After two days in London my shoulders ache from carrying my rucksack; my knees hurt from pounding the pavements. On the Central Line so many of us were crammed into a tunnel on the way to the platform that we came to a standstill. At once I imagined people falling and getting trampled underfoot. I had to say to myself (I hope silently, but I fear I might have whispered it aloud), 'Don't panic, LeFanu, don't panic.' But weirdly, on the Bakerloo Line to Elephant and Castle late on Tuesday morning, on my way to Michèle's for a Group of Three meeting, there were only two of us in the carriage when we arrived at Elephant. The other passenger looked a cheerful, nice, tubby man, then suddenly I thought, What if he's a homicidal maniac? Walking along the empty corridor to the lift I passed an old man creeping along with a stick, and waiting alone by the lift all I could hear, getting nearer and nearer, was tap, tap, tap... I am not usually as paranoid as this. What is happening to me?

Dolores, who has lived, worked, and paid her taxes in this country, married to my brother Julian for nearly fifty years, has just received a 'permanent right of residence'. What a relief. Who would ever have thought, before the xenophobic Tories came to power, such things would be necessary?

22 November

Proofreading *Something of Themselves*, I kept on coming across the word 'alas'. What am I – some kind of corseted Victorian sensation novelist, with the back of my hand held to my brow? I have cut every instance.

At this morning's tai chi workshop Sheila – who suffers from asthma and arthritis but bravely carries on, and whom I consider a tai chi friend – said, during our two-minute banana break, that Corbyn was 'Marxist' and shouldn't be Prime Minister, and that Boris Johnson 'gets things done'. I felt so choked with anger I had to turn and walk away from her. The front page of the *Daily Mail* is screaming 'Marxist' in relation to Labour's manifesto.

2 December

Yesterday, the first day of winter, was cold, still, and bright with sun, after weeks of rain, grey sky, and mud. This morning we had a proper hard frost: silver hedges, golden oaks, scarlet crab apples.

5 December

The index: oh my God, the index! The indexer has made scores of weird choices that I am going to have to challenge, even though the index looks 'finished' because it has already been typeset.

10 December

I had thought that with the index I would just have to check that the page references were correct, and probably do that randomly rather than go through all the hundreds of entries. But no. The indexer has indexed the names of people who are not actually named by me in the book, most of them aristocrats with lengthy names and titles, who appear – fleetingly – in the text as, e.g., General This or That. Looking at the index you get a totally skewed idea of what the book is about – as if it's a compilation of generals in the Victorian British

Army. The indexer has also indexed the names of countries that didn't then exist, such as Mozambique, which appears nowhere in the text, and gives spurious dates for those countries. It is like having extensive footnotes on my text, with information taken from inaccurate sources on the internet.

I became increasingly upset, striking out more and more entries. Then I was filled with a terrible doubt: maybe those entries showed up a lack in my text; or maybe I had completely the wrong idea about indexes, and they were *supposed* to give all these (extraneous) details... But I banished those doubts. It is *my* book. If I had wanted all that commentary, I would have put it in myself. HB cheered me up by reminding me that the job of an index is not to annotate, but to help navigate. It took me three whole days to work my way through it, and I sent off the changes late on Friday. I feel rattled.

However, I was massively encouraged on Sunday night when I got an email from my brother-in-law saying what a great endorsement my book had received from David Kynaston. David Kynaston, author of those social histories of twentieth-century Britain that are so good? What endorsement? I hurriedly went to the Hurst website – and there indeed it splendidly is, as my brother-in-law had so cleverly spotted, right next to the lovely endorsement already given to my book by Lara Feigel. 'Imaginatively conceived, meticulously researched and subtly narrated,' Kynaston has written, '*Something of Themselves* is not only a biographical treasure trove but also offers fresh insights into that charged moment when the writing was at last firmly on the wall for old-style British imperialism.' How incredibly generous. I can feel myself falling in love with him!

And I must record how pleased I was by the indexer's careful indexing of all my references to horses – those poor bloody horses, from England, Ireland, Canada, Australia, hundreds of thousands of them, totally unsuited to the South African terrain, abandoned on battlefields to be pecked to death by vultures.

13 December

A dark day: the sleazebag Johnson has massively increased the number of Tory seats in yesterday's general election, and the Labour Party has lost seats accordingly. The media are saying no one liked Jeremy Corbyn. But why not? Do people really believe that he is a friend of terrorists/a dangerous Marxist/an anti-Semite? (The Chief Rabbi, backed by the BBC on every news and comment programme, urged everyone to vote Tory.) But to vote for Johnson: understandable if you're a property developer, or a banker, or a hedge fund manager, but surely ordinary people don't believe that they will benefit from his government? Well, yes, they must do.

21 December

Winter solstice: sun this morning, rain this afternoon, mud all around.

Suddenly, yesterday, Daisy Leitch, the Hurst production director, emailed me to ask if I could produce a title and credit for the cover image? No, I couldn't. She went to the designer, and the title came back: 'a boer burning'. But I didn't have time to check my emails again until late in the evening. When I did, I replied at once: 'Capital B Boer, and surely "burning Boer farm"?' But is it too late? Has the whole thing been sent to the printers?

I woke this morning at 5am with a dreadful sinking feeling in my stomach. What about the pictures of Kipling and Conan Doyle that are also on the cover, the sketches by Mortimer Menpes? They haven't been credited either; of course they should be. The Kingsley portrait is not so much of a problem as it is the same one as is reproduced inside, where it is credited in the list of illustrations.

But *not* Menpes's sketches of Kipling and Conan Doyle. A sick panic washed over me.

I emailed Daisy first thing, but have had no reply, as indeed I haven't had a reply to my correction regarding the 'burning Boer farm'. She may well have gone off for Christmas. Farhaana has been away all week and will not be back until after Christmas. And I'm thinking, Is the cover really my responsibility? Shouldn't someone in the office have noticed? And once again I am revisiting: the book is finished, done, signed off…and then suddenly here it is back again.

22 December

Email from Daisy: all the cover corrections done, credits added, and 'I am just running a final check on the text (running heads, correlation of numbers on Contents page, that sort of thing) and will send to press so the printer has it tomorrow morning.' Thank you, Daisy!

Coda

15 January 2020

The results of Monday's blood test came back: ESR 24, and a message from the surgery to make a telephone appointment with one of the doctors to discuss a possible increase in steroid dosage. Well, I don't want to increase the dose, and although the pain in my hips and buttocks is severe in the mornings, it does wear off over the course of the day. It is nothing like as crippling as it was last summer, when my ESR was 60. I think I can manage this – with the help of paracetamol – and would like if possible to drop another 1 milligram of prednisolone and get down to 9 milligrams.

So I rang the surgery to arrange to talk to lovely Dr Davies. Last time I saw him he told me sorrowfully that we (he and I together!) just couldn't expect to be free of all aches and pains at our age, irrespective of the PMR.

'Dr Davies?' said the receptionist. 'Hmm, I think he's left.'

'Left? Retired, you mean?'

She wasn't going to be drawn on that one. And then I remembered: I have never seen a photo of Dr Davies on the surgery noticeboard, where all the doctors and other practice staff have their photos up like a medical family tree. His presence in the practice has always been a bit…shadowy. On past occasions I've had to inform the receptionist (who apparently didn't recognize his name) that he works mainly in Pudding Pie Lane. And now I'm wondering whether he isn't an avatar of Dr Pahl, the handsome Indian doctor/god who first diagnosed my PMR back in 2016, and whom I have never set eyes on again. If, like Dr Pahl, Dr Davies comes from another realm, perhaps his vanishing now is a sign that his work with me is done; that this year, 2020, will at last see my release from the talons of PMR.

1 February

Britain left the European Union last night, at 11pm. I couldn't bear to watch any of it on TV: too much crowing from Tory Brexiters. Thank God our horrible PM failed to get his wish to have Big Ben ring out a celebratory peal of bells. On Wednesday night the British MEPs left the EU building for the last time. Led by Nigel Farage, and including ghastly Ann Widdecombe, and Claire Fox who really should know better, they had taken out Union Jacks in the debating chamber and waved them triumphantly above their heads, grinning and cavorting.

I thought of the rioters in the streets of London and other towns when news came in May 1900 of the Relief of Mafeking. 'Mother, may I go and maffick, / Tear around and hinder traffic?' wrote the sardonic Saki, who had been writing a satirical column on warmongering politicians since the beginning of the war. Kipling, returned from South Africa and living in Rottingdean, boasted of instigating a 'merry little riot' in the village. His aunt Georgie Burne-Jones, on the other side of the village green, must have been appalled. She (like Mary Doyle, Arthur's mother) was resolutely anti-war. When, two years later, the war was brought to an end with the signing of the Treaty of Vereeniging, she hung a black banner out of the windows of North End House with the words 'WE HAVE KILLED AND ALSO TAKEN POSSESSION' painted on it in large white capitals.

In 1900 our European neighbours viewed the Mafeking riots with barely disguised incredulity and horror. On Wednesday night all the European MEPs and Ministers who were interviewed expressed their sorrow with grave courtesy. I felt ashamed to be British.

6 February

Publication day! Hurst have done me proud with an astonishingly handsome book: blue binding, red stitching, quality paper, colour illustrations. It is absolutely beautiful.

I have had congratulatory emails from Rhianna Louise, publicist at Hurst, and from Julia in Sosnowiec; and from Michèle, a lovely spotted Joules dress by special delivery.

A ground frost this morning: a thin layer of ice on the puddles, the sun is shining, and the birds are singing. Earlier I saw the two jackdaws, a jay, *and* the woodpecker swarming around the bird table.

17 February

Last Wednesday I gave my talk to the Kipling Society in the Royal Over-Seas League. First I had tea with Rhianna – whom I was meeting for the first time – in the League's elegant tea room that overlooks Green Park, and then we made our way up an elegant curved, wide-stepped staircase to the meeting room. I was warmly welcomed by Mike Kipling; by Alex Bubb, who organizes the meetings; and by someone who used to live round the corner from Mum and Dad in Cloudesley Road. At the end of my talk ('Kipling in Bloemfontein') one or two of the senior members obviously wanted to test my more general Kipling knowledge – I believe I passed the test. Today I received an email from Mike telling me that a number of people had told him it was the 'most informed and entertaining talk' they had attended in years.

The following evening James threw a party for me at the Academy Club – with champagne and delicious canapés – and it was just lovely. Mon gave a wonderful talk about our work in South Africa, and how closely the South Africa of the days that I was researching informs the South Africa of today. She recounted some Simon's Town anecdotes (kindly not mentioning the occasion when I led her on a wild goose chase in search of the Palace Barracks Hospital, when there it was, opposite the railway station, the whole time), and said how much she enjoyed the detective work… Mon is brilliant. There was only one uninvited guest: a man with a small dog. Then about eighteen of us went round the corner to have dinner at Masala Zone – cleverly pre-ordered by James – and we sat at two long tables in a large, sunken alcove or cave, and it was very jolly. Jill's Lily and Jesse came with us, so along with Ismay, HB and J there were enough young people to offset us oldies. Later we returned to the good old Earl's Court Premier Inn, which is getting to be a home from home.

So go, little book (or, in truth, quite big book), launched into the world by my good publishers and my good friends. Go, with your hair brushed, your face washed, your coat buttoned and your shoelaces tied, and may the world make of you what it will. I have done all I can for you.

9 781800 422629